COLLEGE SWIMMING COACH

Social Issue And Worlds

Donald W. Hastings
University of Tennessee

UNIVERSITY
PRESS OF
AMERICA

LANHAM • NEW YORK • LONDON

Copyright © 1987 by

University Press of America,® Inc.

4720 Boston Way
Lanham, MD 20706

3 Henrietta Street
London WC2E 8LU England

British Cataloging in Publication Information Available

Library of Congress Cataloging-in-Publication Data

Hastings, Donald W., 1940-
College swimming coach.

Bibliography: p.
Includes indexes.
1. Swimming—Coaching—Vocational guidance—United
States.   2. College sports—United States—Coaching.
3. Swimming—United States—Coaches—Social conditions.
I. Title.
GV837.65.H37   1987   797.2'102373   87-21580
ISBN 0-8191-6628-6 (alk. paper)
ISBN 0-8191-6629-4 (pbk. : alk. paper)

All University Press of America books are produced on acid-free
paper which exceeds the minimum standards set by the National
Historical Publication and Records Commission.

Connie, Peter, and Laura

ACKNOWLEDGMENTS

I want to express my appreciation to those members of the academic community who excused me from the onerous task of committee work and provided release time in order for me to continue coaching full-time when it became necessary. I also would like to thank the administrators, coaches, and support staff in the university athletic and sports community for their help and for the opportunity to become involved as a working member of their program. It was an experience on which I will always reflect with fondness and pleasure.

I wish to thank Professors James A. Black, Brenda Phillips, Joy T. De Sensi, and Craig A. Wrisberg for their insights and helpful comments on an earlier draft of the manuscript. I also would like to thank them for allowing me access to their personal libraries to borrow materials and volumes not available elsewhere.

My special thanks go to T.C. Carlisle for letting me sign on as a volunteer coach and for providing valuable insights as a mentor and reviewer of various manuscripts over the years. I also wish to express my gratitude to Ray Bussard for helpful hints on teaching swimming techniques and for the chance to be the oldest age grouper in summer camp. To Joe Gentry, my thanks are extended for permitting me to work with the age-groupers, for his helpful hints on "style" (tips on how to improve as a deck coach), and for his comments on the manuscript.

As usual, the author is solely responsible for any sins of omission or commission.

TABLE OF CONTENTS

PREFACE

First, this book is aimed at the practitioner, the physical education student or student of swimming who anticipates a career in coaching. For this reader the book provides a practical overview and guide to the activities expected of the college swim coach at various stages during a career. Second, this book also is useful for the behavioral scientist. For the sport sociologist it is a case study of the socialization of an individual into the position of swim coach. For the student of occupations and organizations the volume serves as an illustration of an apprenticeship occupation, since the various roles and responsibilities of the intercollegiate swim coach are identified and the various activities expected while learning a career are described. This book provides an practical introduction to the social roles of swim coach, not treated systematically anywhere else in the literature on sport, occupations, psychology, or sociology.

The materials for this volume are based on personal experience. While teaching sociology I worked as a volunteer swim coach. After a few years I moved to a position of associate coach with a joint appointment between the sociology and athletics department. Later I served a brief stint as an interim co-head coach. Currently, I am back in the classroom during the day and coaching age-groupers at night.

Although I swam in a collegiate program that now is classified as NCAA Division III, my experiences with coaching have been at the Division I level. The bias of this book is clearly toward programs that strive to be highly competitive, that offer scholarships, and that must compete with the major money making, high visibility sports. Many of the problems confronted in Division I program are duplicated in Division II and III programs. Unfortunately some of the frustrations and problems of the smaller programs with fewer personnel and smaller budgets no doubt are overlooked. The oversight is neither intentional, nor meant to belittle these programs; it simply stems from a lack of personal experience in these settings.

Another bias in this work is the infrequent mention of diving. Clearly swimming and diving are dual elements of a program. Typically, the head coach oversees the swimming part of the program and delegates authority for running the diving part of the program to a diving coach (either a head diving coach or an assistant coach). An effort may be made to ensure that swimmers and divers act as a team, or in some cases the swimmers and divers may only get together when it is time to join for competition. In still other cases the head coach is responsible for both swimming and diving. Since the programs with which I have the most familiarity tend to be administered by the head coach and have a diving coach as an assistant, I tend to treat the problems of the diving program as separate items unless they directly affect the head coach.

The bases for my observations in this book are twofold. First is a lifetime of involvement in swimming, initially as an age-grouper, then as a high school and collegiate swimmer, and more recently as a Masters swimmer and as a coach. These different roles provide a range of experiences from which to draw. Informal conversations with swimmers, parents, other coaches and members of the swimming community have provided valuable insights on the process of becoming a mentor accepted by swimmers and by the larger sports community.

Second, as a sociologist/coach I have reviewed the literature in sport sociology and in swimming in order to sketch a framework which makes interpretable my observations both theoretically and practically. The perspective used to describe the social world of the collegiate swim coach is that of the sociologist. Any vocabulary terms that might be unfamiliar to the reader are defined. In general the terms are made clear by the context in which they are used. The perspective presented in this book represents only one individual's interpretation of the social world of the collegiate swim coach. Other observers no doubt would see and report it differently. To ensure that this interpretation is an accurate reflection of the social world of the college swim coach I persuaded a few swimmers, coaches, and colleagues to read and comment critically on various drafts of the manuscript. My apologies for disturbing their wa (sense of harmony and well-being). Hopefully this volume will prove to be informative, a fair reading of the roles of the coach, and perhaps useful to the behavioral scientist and the future coach.

This book does not feature information that is technique-oriented. Such information is covered in much more detail in textbooks on swimming and in the professional swimming journals. Nor is this a manual on how to create workouts. There are a number of fine books on this topic already in print. Also this book does not focus on all aspects of the coach's role of interacting with the swimmer. Topics covering goal setting, mental programming, communication, and motivation are left to the sports psychologists. There a number of works on various dimensions of these topics currently available.

The primary concern of this manuscript is the social world of swimming coach. Attention is paid to the nature of the job as an apprenticeship occupation, as an occupation striving to establish a professional identity, and as a social role important in building personal identity among one's peers, members of the community, and for posterity. The role of the assistant coach, volunteer or paid, is described. The process of becoming a the head coach is reviewed by looking at the advertisements for a college or university coaching position and interpreting the job requirements. The kinds of issues to which the applicant and the athletic director are sensitive also are examined. The various roles that the coach plays in interacting with key people inside and outside the sports community are identified. Some of the role conflicts and pressures faced by the coach are described as are some of the strategies to escape these tensions. In the latter part of the work some of the possible decision making strategies and some of issues that need to be handled by the coach are analyzed. Those issues receiving particular attention are the process of recruiting and the challenge of building support within the academic community and the community at large.

CHAPTER 1.—OVERVIEW AND KEY CONCEPTS

Introduction

In the modern world sports are ever present. We participate in them sometimes willingly and sometimes not so willingly. We attend contests in person. We watch them from the comfort of our homes. We read about them in the mass media. The world of sport impinges on our consciousness from cradle to grave. Sports affect the values we learn, the feelings of identity with the "team," the desire to express joy, sorrow, or aggression. People learn to want to participate in physical activity, to compete, to gamble, or to get high from "doing." Some individuals may simply wish to dabble, others to become professionals, eventually emulating one of the "greats" either as an athlete or a coach. Some may wish to avoid sports altogether. Each of these effects of sports participation are topics which capture the attention of students of sport.

Relatively little discussion is found on the social world of the coach despite a growing body of literature on entry into sport by athletes and participants, on the study of kinds of social learning they experience, and on the types of roles that athletes play in the world of sport. Much of what sport sociologists know of the coaching profession rests on the experiences of football, basketball, baseball, and hockey coaches; the social world of major sports marked by high media visibility and money-making enterprises (Massengale 1974; Sabock 1973; Sage 1974; 1975b; and 1980). The social world of the coach in low visibility sports and non-money-making sports usually receives little attention.

The social world of the college swim coach has been by-passed as a topic of study. This book moves to compensate for this oversight. Various aspects of learning the roles of the swim coach are examined as an individual moves through the progression from volunteer coach, to assistant coach, and finally, to head coach. The stages of learning in coaching, an "apprenticeship" occupation, are also identified. Issues involved in the hiring of a coach are discussed. The major role clusters of organization and communication are reviewed. Finally, particular attention is paid to how the coach relates to key people in the athletic department, sports community, and college and university as well as others outside the world of sport.

Coaching as a career

Entry and stages of socialization.- Coaching is a job. It involves a bundle of activities for which the individual receives remuneration (Hughes 1951). It also is a career in that the individual participates in the labor force for an identifiable period of time. The career is bounded by entry and retirement. A career has a shape--path, line or trajectory--in which performance usually is assumed to be at least in part a function of age (Glasser and Strauss 1971). Excellence in performance of job activities is rewarded not only through pay but also through esteem from fellow workers and prestige from outsiders. Generally as one ages, one gains more skills, expertise, and status.

Entry into coaching usually follows one of two major avenues: (1) individuals move from a role of primary involvement in sport as swimmer into coaching, a direct production role; or (2) move from a role of consumer, either direct or indirect into coaching. (See Loy, McPherson, and Kenyon 1978: 17-20.)[1] Regardless of which path an individual takes in moving into coaching,[2] once having entered the position, learning how to coach begins.

There are four stages of learning in developing a career as coach.

1. Anticipatory socialization.-This stage of learning involves the development of understandings from afar of what coaches do--how do they behave, what values are espoused, and what skills are required? For instance, does the coach convey the impression of confidence and knowledgeability of sport; use the rhetoric of the sport properly; impress one as a good manager; and present a public image as articulate and a good representative of the institution? Often these understandings are stereotypical, mythical creations of media representatives from the institution, or misperceptions based on observations made as an outsider. In some cases, these perceptions are derived while one participates in the sport.[3]

2. Apprenticeship.-The assistant coach during an apprenticeship learns a variety of role responsibilities. These lessons serve as the basis for gaining credentials, experience, and a reputation for eventually being hired or appointed as a head coach. The neophyte must be led before becoming a leader. An individual must serve as a trainee in order to pick up

the lore, myths, and skills that comprise the world of competitive swimming before becoming a head coach. Serving as an apprentice means the individual is involved in on-the-job training. Apprenticeship involves learning the basic understandings that govern practical ways of doing things in the day-to-day routine of the job. Classrooms may teach the principles underpinning activities, (physiology, principles of motor behavior, nutrition, psychology of coaching, and management theory) but becoming a successful practitioner is obtained through actual experience.

3. Institutional socialization.-Stevenson (1976b: 65-76) hypothesized that people believe that participation in college and university sports leads to the acquisition of moral values, character traits, and skills that transfer to non-sport settings. Further, he hypothesized that people believe that participation in sports facilitates getting jobs outside of sport. These products of learning through sports participation are examples of institutional socialization. Stevenson (1976a: 1-8) found that people endorsed the belief that sport is an arena in which moral training occurs, but did not see participation in sport as helpful in obtaining a job in medicine, law, or business. Stevenson (1976b: 65-76) in passing suggested that the transferability of values and skills probably is more readily accomplished in moves between like situations (sport to sport settings). After all, analogues are more apt to be recognized in circumstances where past experiences are repeated rather than in new and strange settings.

People presume that a swimmer or a coach who is a participant in a particular program will acquire skills as well as some of the philosophy of the program. They assume that both technical and moral training occur in any program, but that certain programs are more meritorious than others as places for the apprentice to pick up new techniques and principles of organization, especially if the programs are successful. A survey of coaches asking them to identify which programs they would recommend to an apprentice no doubt would quickly reveal the pecking order among institutions.

People inside and outside of the world of sport-- and especially the swimming community--take for granted that the apprentice will acquire a body of technical skills. More problematic is the presumption that a particular set of values has been learned. People inside of the world of sport and swimming when interacting with "alumni of particular programs" take these "learned values" as hypothetical traits to be quickly verified as present or absent. People are generally quicker to "read" a particular "attitude" as present or absent from the other person's character and slower to "reject" the other's claim of "expertise." Persons holding credentials or possessing a reputation are provided with an additional layer of protection from possible devaluation. After all, there is a professional organization of coaches that legitimizes the claim of the individual.[4]   After having served as an apprentice and having begun to build a reputation as a coach the individual seeks to become a head coach.

4. Professionalization.-In this stage the individual develops competency as a head coach with the ability to assume full responsibilities for organizing and administrating a program. Along with the position and its associated prestige go the risks of failure and loss of job. Those who have worked as a coach and experienced the pressures and frustration may be accepted by other members of the coaching community. Once having coached, accreditation may be applied for as a member of the American Swim Coaches Association (ASCA).

Certification and accountability.- Coaching, like many other occupations in which a greater part of the body of knowledge is accumulated through on-the-job experience and a lesser part through formal education and clinics, faces the problems of defining who is a professional, handling certification, and fixing accountability. Coaches claim a mastery over a body of knowledge that others do not necessarily have. They also claim expertise in the application of that knowledge and the teaching of certain skills. They expect that people both inside and outside of the swimming community accept their identity as "coach." Further, coaches expect their actions to be evaluated by peers and outsiders, accruing esteem from their peers and prestige from outsiders for honors earned and misfortunes suffered.[5]

A classic strategy used by people in an occupation to gain professional identity is to set up a professional organization, institute a system of credentials, and require the membership to acquire certification. In 1984, U.S. Swimming directed that a certification program be outlined. It was developed in February 1985, approved by the ASCA in April 1985, accepted applications for membership and accreditation as of October 1985, and became officially installed as a system on January 1, 1986. All U.S. Swimming coaches will require membership and accreditation after January 1, 1988. After that date, anyone who holds a membership card is, from the stance of the ASCA, "licensed" to coach. (Should these credentials be tested and upheld in a court of law, all the trappings of a profession will have been acquired.)

According to ASCA, "The goal of the certification program is: to provide a nationally recognized method of identifying professionally prepared swimming coaches" (ASCA 1985: 1). By delineating standards for knowledge mastered and experience gained, principles of inclusion and exclusion are fixed for entry into a membership of professional coaches. Level of achievement, degree of knowledge, and extent of experience provide three ranking systems for assigning levels of professional esteem. In short, certification defines who is a coach, creates a structure for coaching, and provides a ladder for professional advancement (ASCA 1985: 2). Certification is also a standard by which performance may be judged and accountability assigned. (For a definition of accountability, see Betz 1981.) On the one hand, certification establishes standards for employment. Employers can identify the "type of coach" they want to hire. Employers can obtain employment records and a verification of credentials from the ASCA national office in Ft. Lauderdale, FL. Coaches can use the ASCA employment service in looking for jobs. Credentials also may be used as evidence of career development and as a basis for arguing for pay raises (Anselmi 1986:25). On the other hand, certification may be taken as proof of expertise when assigning risks of insurability or proving negligence and incompetency in legal actions. For instance, after January 1988, coaches are expected to take the Red Cross Coaches Safety Training Program every 3 years and re-validate CPR training annually.

The ASCA credentials system evaluates three areas of behavior. First is achievement. The coaching record is judged by the performance of individual swimmers. Did any swimmers earn the position of High School All-American, Prep-School All-American, YMCA All-American, NCAA II or III All-American, Junior College All-American, NAIA All-American, U.S. Swimming Junior National Qualifier, U.S. Swimming Top 16 National Age Grouper, Senior US Swimming Qualifier or NCAA I Qualifier? Has the coach satisfied requirements for making the "international trip list?"

Second is _education_. The coach's academic record is reviewed. Formal course work is evaluated by looking at the credit hours taken and the nature of degrees earned (sport-focused, sport-related, or general education). Clinics attended are judged for the calibre of instruction (the instructors' certifications and ASCA recognized expertise, the duration of each session, and whether the clinic is ASCA sanctioned).

Third is _experience_. The coach's on-the-job experience as an intern, assistant coach, and head coach is reviewed.

Certification reports two items: (1) level of achievement-ranked levels 1 through 5--lowest to highest; and (2) total units--which combines units awarded for education and for experience. The actual calculation of units for each of these areas of activity is far too complicated to present here. (See the finals 1985 for the details. Interestingly, the Canadians first used a certification process and a standardized examination to establish levels of competency.) The ASCA, upon completing the certification process, sends a certificate and identification card to each registered coach. The certificate can be mounted as a plaque and publicly displayed or filed depending on the whims of the coach. For those who display the plaque, it becomes a statement of progress as validated by one's peers, part of one's role identity. Certificates, awards, and photographs of dignitaries with inscriptions addressed to the coach that bedeck the coach's office walls confirm the individual's self image as "coach" and verify for any visitor that a larger audience of notables inside the social world of sport and among the public at large recognize the coach and his/her feats accomplished. As the number of mementos increase and more wall space is used, the coach's public image is expanded and enhanced. This practice is so ingrained among coaches that visitors and athletes expect the display of such trappings of office. If a coach chooses not to follow this custom, the visitors and athletes may assume something is amiss, wonder about his/her credentials and the amount of experience. Certificates and memorabilia may be collected in anticipation of one's later years after leaving the world of sport; collecting is important to the creation of a "post-self" (Schmitt and Leonard 1986).

Role identity.- A role identity is "the character ...that an individual devises ...as an occupant of a particular social position...." [It is the] ..." imaginative view of himself as he likes to think of himself being and acting as an occupant of that position" (McCall and Simmons 1978: 65). Thus, an individual who occupies the position of coach may see the job as work with all its trappings (source of money, prestige, worth to others, and meaning for being an individual) or as avocation seen as something other than work, separate, subordinate, pleasurable, and meaningful. Although the position may be seen as either work or avocation, elements of both may be important to the individual in shaping a role-identity. Where work elements predominate, the role identity will probably emphasize professionalism. Alternatively, where avocational elements hold sway, the role identity will probably stress leisure. For the assistant who views apprenticeship as a stepping stone to the position of head coach, the job probably is accepted as part of an emerging professional role-identity. For the volunteer who is coaching for fun or to escape from the pressures of work, the position probably enriches the role-identity of the "serious amateur"--the devotee (Stebbins 1979). In some instances, a professional identity may be forsaken due to job burn-out, failure, or perhaps personal crises such as divorce or loss of a loved one that cause one to re-think what a job means.[6]

Post-self.- Some social psychologists suggest that athletes and, by extension, coaches see their acts, actions, or accomplishments as ways to create a "post-self...the concern of a person with the presentation of his or her self in history" (Schmitt and Leonard 1986: 1088). In everyday terms coaches want to "leave a mark," "want to be remembered," "want to gain a bit of immortality," or "go down in history," for a winning tradition, winning a championship, for coaching the Olympic team, making the Hall of Fame, or less dramatically, teaching skills or character to their athletes. Apparently, participation simply is not enough. One's present actions anticipate a future that will recall an important past. The coach as a historical figure becomes an identity against which future coaches judge themselves. Deeds become standards to emulate or surpass. For the coach creating this future identity, current deeds are recognized with prizes, trophies, and certifications. These are the memorabilia over which participants can reminisce and the standards to which neophytes can aspire. Coaches want to be viewed and recalled favorably as heroes and heroines, not goats. The image

7

that they create is not only a product of their own actions, but the collective evaluation of the athletes and other key people in the sports community. The present generation of sports fans and personalities validates or vilifies the feat, records it, and enshrines it for future generations to worship or mock.

The formation and recognition of role identity--past, present or future--becomes a conscious issue only in those fleeting moments of reflection and recollection. Similarly, coaches do not currently appear to be overly concerned with the issue of credentials, since the system is just beginning. Credentials in effect are based on what the elite coaches have accomplished in their careers. Their accomplishments serve as the standards for others to follow. The longer the credentials system is in operation, the greater the number of coaches who will use certifications levels as another item in their resumes. Coaches will recognize on which of the three measures they are strong or weak, and no doubt will move to broaden their base of professional expertise.

Currently those individuals who are in the swimming community or are knowledgeable about it are able to identify coaches within their network who have reputations as good age group, YMCA, or collegiate coaches. Beyond the swimming community coaching visibility is quite limited. At best some people may be able to identify some of the elite coaches who have headed or served on an Olympic team, or won an NCAA championship, or are affiliated with the local school in the community. Whether evaluators are insiders to the swimming community or outsiders, they typically rely on the traditional criteria for a job: education, experience, and record to date. They also evaluate the kinds of experiences coaches have had, looking at the programs in which they trained or assumed major responsibilities as athlete or coach. (Incidentally, unless an athletic director, an insider to sport, has had experience in coaching swimming or has developed a feeling for the problems of coaches over the years, the athletic director [AD] probably will use these criteria in evaluating job applicants for the head coaching job or in deciding to keep the head coach as part of the coaching staff.)

Other concepts.- Professional legitimacy for a coach is based on formal and informal criteria. Formal criteria include educational experience and credentials. Informal criteria include the reputation of the coach and the program with which an individual served an apprenticeship as well as the individual's own reputation. Both sets of criteria come into play when the athletic director hires a new head coach or when the head coach adds volunteers or paid assistants to the coaching staff. The formal and informal criteria that usually appear in job descriptions are called job markers.

The coach occupies a social position. Attached to that position is a social script of how the coach is expected to behave or act. This script is called a role definition, the behavior as played out is the role performance.

Most positions have multiple roles. Combinations of skills, tasks, activities, and responsibilities that must be fulfilled by a job holder are called role clusters. Coaching is no different. One important role cluster for the coach is the organizational role which involves technical and managerial skills. Acting in a managerial capacity, the coach must administer personnel who are part of the program, must plan and organize the program's agenda, must handle the budget, and must oversee the clerical work. How the managerial responsibilities are organized and executed is dependent on the coach's technical knowledge and skills acquired through formal education and service as an apprentice. A second important role cluster is the communication role. Here the coach should be sensitive to styles of communication (recognizing that both verbal and non-verbal parts of the message influence the efficacy of one's performance) as well as the settings where coach and swimmer interact.

The head coach as organizer and communicator will effect a particular decision making style which ranges from autocratic--where the coach makes all the decisions, through delegative--where the coach assigns a decision to a subordinate and acts to implement that decision, to consultative--where the coach shares problems with swimmers and staff, seeking input, then making a decision and participative--where the coach talks to all parties collectively and individually and everyone votes. Which style is selected by a coach and how much control one wishes to exercise are important factors in structuring the program and shaping relationships between the coaching staff and athletes. The head coach's approach to the program will depend on the philosophy of management, whether it is product-oriented--trying to produce as many elite swimmers as possible or person-oriented--trying to produce a swimmer who is mechanically sound and seeks to develop the whole personality. How the head coach chooses to run a program is reflected in the <u>process of recruiting</u>. Ideally, recruiting should be sensitive to producing a group of individuals where there is compatibility between coach and athletes, or between coaching staff and athletes.

The coach's style of leadership also affects social relationships with other individuals inside and outside of the sport community. Within the sport community the coach's role definitions and performances are examined based on interacting with the individuals inside the athletic department and outside of it. Insiders include the AD, sports information representatives, team physician, the trainer, aquatics director, academic advisor, and secretarial and janitorial staff. Additional insiders are other coaches, adult and student boosters, other teams on campus, parents, and representatives from the conference, NCAA, and ASCA.

Since coaches move from one organizational setting to another and each setting involves a variety of possible social relationships, it is easy to imagine that an actor may occupy two or more positions whose role definitions, when juxtaposed make contradictory demands. When a coach is caught in a set of cross-pressures acting in the roles of coach and family person or coach and teacher/professor, this is <u>role conflict</u>. In some circumstances an actor feels increased pressure in fulfilling the expectations attached to a role. This is called <u>role strain</u>. For instance, a coach may face pressures from others (the faculty, administration, students, or athlete) to perform better; this is role strain.

Various strategies for handling role strain and role conflict often are employed to maintain a sense of balance in everyday life. These various concepts and issues will be addressed as the social world and roles of collegiate swim coach are explored in this book.

Summary

--Sports in the modern world are ubiquitous. Despite the coverage given to coaches in major sports, little is known of the social world and roles of the collegiate swim coach, as a mentor in a minor sport.

--Coaching is a career. Learning to become a coach involves four steps--anticipatory socialization, apprenticeship, institutional socialization, and professionalization.

--A coach's role identity is tied to a personal orientation toward the activity, viewed as either work or leisure. How the coach presents himself or herself to others depends on how one envisions a post-self.

--Getting hired demands that a coach possess the appropriate credentials. Once hired the coach is administrator and teacher who must establish a viable set of social relationships with people inside and outside of the world of sport. These ties often involve role strain or role conflict with which the coach must learn to cope or eventually be forced to withdraw from the job.

REVIEW QUESTIONS

1. What is a career? What are the stages of socialization into a career?

2. What is certification? What organization certifies the coach's credentials? How does the organization assist a coach once certified?

3. What is meant by role identity? Do you see coaching as a professional activity or a leisure time activity?

4. What is meant by the term post-self? What kind of record or legacy do you want to leave for future generations?

NOTES

1   According to Loy et al. (1978: 17-20) primary
involvement involves "actual participation in the game
or sport as a player or contestant;" "secondary
involvement refers to all other forms of
participation." This latter category is subdivided
into direct producers who "perform tasks that have
direct consequences for the outcome of the game" and
indirect producers "whose activities have no direct
consequences for the outcome of a sport event."
Consumers are differentiated as direct--attenders of
the event, and indirect--viewers of media.

2   Unfortunately, to date there are no systematic
studies of job mobility of swimming coaches. Various
combinations of characteristics (which appear below)
should be investigated in order to ascertain the
backgrounds of college swimming coaches. There are a
number of paths possible to follow in becoming a head
coach. What the weights are among the other
characteristics has yet to be ascertained. Possible
background characteristics linked to entry into college
coaching include:

Swimming background   (in addition to competitive
swimming, water polo, and synchronized swimming)
1. Yes as:
        a. Age-grouper--YMCA and/or U.S. Swimming
        b. High school or Prep school
        c. Junior college
        d. College/University
        e. National/International
        f. Masters
        g. Professional, marathons
2. No

Formal education
1. Attended college, but did not finish
2. Bachelor's
3. Master's
4. Doctorate

Major
1. Physical education
2. Other

Assistant experience
1. Yes as:
        a. Volunteer
        b. Paid-part time
        c. Paid-full time

13

2. No

Coaching experience
1. Works in categories 1a, 1b, or 1f
2. Split assignment--coach in sport other than swimming as well as a swimming coach
3. Coach/teacher or professor

3 I suspect that stereotypes are developed while one occupies roles other than one of primary involvement. These stereotypes tend to be based on understandings of what coaches do in the money-making and high media visibility sports, like football, baseball, and basketball, rather than the actions of coaches in non-money-making, low visibility minor sports. Stereotypes are formed by watching the coaches actions while attending a contest, watching on television, or serving as an official. I assume that people assign a combination of traits to coaches which remains relatively constant regardless of the sport. These traits might include the ability to get along with people, to motivate, to maintain control, or to evaluate skill levels of athletes.

4 Interestingly, once an individual's expertise is questioned, there is a tendency to devalue other aspects of character. If important attitude traits are read as missing and these traits are taken as essential to the character of the individual, then others may actively challenge one's claims of expertise whether warranted or not. To prevent an individual from occupying an office, others simply need raise questions on the suitability of the attitudes espoused and/or alleged competency. Whether these queries are vaguely or sharply put, matters little. The fact they are raised at all, jeopardizes the acceptability of the individual for the job. Incidentally, character assassination becomes a device for wresting control from an individual in a position of authority. Once the moral character of the office holder has been devalued, that individual has no legitimate claim for remaining in office (See Goffman 1967).

5 Some commentators claim that evaluation is mandatory given the nature of competition in two-party settings. Dual meets are zero-sum games, one party wins, the other loses. Winning equals success, losing is failure. Success is lauded, failure gains ignominy.

6 One strategy of coping with stress is to substitute a leisure identity, using recreation, entertainment, or

sport as a crutch to get through the crisis. Occasionally the leisure identity may get transformed into a new professional identity (Kelly 1983).

"Coach, may I have a minute of your time?" (Susan)
"Sure, come on in. What can I do for you?"
"Coach, I'm a phys. ed. major in my junior year.
I need to assist a coach in some sport as part of
my field placement requirement. I was wondering if
you had an opening?" (Susan)
"I have an opening. But why did you choose
swimming rather than basketball or volleyball?"
"I swam as an age-grouper and in high school. I
had a scholarship to swim at the Univ. of X, but
got injured in a car accident at the end of my
sophomore year. I lost too much time trying to
rehabilitate. I gave up my scholarship and
transferred here because it is cheaper." (Susan)
"So, you swam with John Rex? That is good. Do
you want to end up as a head coach in swimming?"
"Coach, right now I think that I would like to
teach and coach in high school. If I can
eventually get a job as a college coach, I'll take
it." (Susan)
"Fine. Why don't we get together next week and
talk about the program."

****

Motives for entering coaching generally fall into
two categories. First are structural motives--an
individual's position in an organization or obligations
to others compel the individual to serve as coach or
pressure the individual to act as a volunteer coach.
For example, teachers may serve as coaches because the
school principal asked them to do so until such time
someone is hired who is more qualified. Or an
individual who is a parent with children who swim in
the program may volunteer as an assistant coach.
Second are personal motives--an individual holds
beliefs or values that can be fulfilled as a coach.
Examples of personal motives are wide ranging and
include ones such as swimming is fun; or it is a great
sport, one in which the individual can learn survival
skills, achieve physical fitness, or learn the "ecstasy
of victory" and the "agony of defeat." Individuals may
view coaching as an extension of a life-long
involvement in sport. Males are more likely to see
coaching as a more viable career choice than females.
Coaching may be a way of earning one's place in
history. Similarly, the excitement of sport, the
immediacy of gratification in teaching others a new
skill, and the sociability and fun of being with others

17

who share similar values are some of the reasons for coaching.

Individuals who enter coaching for structural motives generally have shorter careers than those who enter for individual motives. People who coach due to structural obligations are more likely to withdraw from coaching once those obligations are fulfilled than they are to continue in the position. For instance, a parent probably will not feel compelled to coach after the children have left age-group swimming and moved on to college or have withdrawn from swimming in favor of some other activity. Conversely, individuals who enter coaching for personal motives are more likely to stay as long as the job provides the satisfactions sought. Once the job ceases to satisfy those needs, disenchantment, burnout, and withdrawal may occur.

Whatever a person's motives for entering coaching, the act of starting may be either carefully planned or completely fortuitous. On the one hand, a youth may envision the day of achieving a place in the Swimming Hall of Fame as both swimmer and coach following a glorious career. On the other hand, an individual serving as an assistant never can anticipate whether the head coach will have an indiscreet affair, suffer a stroke, or get fired.

Given the nature of job contracts in college coaching (which usually are one year at a time with no tenure) and the untold events which can and do occur in academic and sports communities on college campuses, it is small wonder that more job openings do not occur every year than do.

Before a neophyte is competent to play the role of coach and be recognized by others as the "coach," one must serve as an apprentice. This position of assistant coach is the first rung on the career ladder for a professional coach.

The apprenticeship role

The apprenticeship role involves learning not only "formal skills," but also the "casual learning of the routine way of whatever" coaches do. (Unfortunately, the sociology of occupations and work is limited in the availability of case studies on apprenticeship jobs, the quoted material and the framework for discussing the apprenticeship role is based on Becker 1972.) It provides the beginner with the opportunity to become familiar with "the sights, sounds, situations, activities, and problems" faced as long as one in involved in the job. The apprentice sees the complexities of formal social relationships between others and the coach. The apprentice also experiences the demands and constraints arising in peer relationships.

The apprentice is involved in the immediate flow of activities. The apprentice picks up knowledge piecemeal, selectively focuses on some activity, value, or skill sequence; analyzing it; and, fitting that item into one's over-all understanding of what is required by the job. The individual picks up skills, lore, and understandings of interactions at his/her own pace. The individual must learn to evaluate competing sets of instructions given by fellow workers on how to best accomplish a task. The apprentice evolves a personalized curriculum of learning within the broader structure of job activities.

The apprentice must recognize that the coach's time and attention are not automatically guaranteed. Learning is a by-product of self-initiative. Learning is active, rather than passive. The coach is not responsible for the apprentice's failure to learn or remain in the job, although the apprentice often wants more structure and guidance from the coach.

Opportunities for learning on-the-job depend on the amount of latitude granted by the head coach and the staff. There is a great deal of variation across programs. Some coaches go to great pains to make sure that the apprentice receives detailed instructions. Other coaches assume that any individual worthy of becoming a coach will become attuned to what is expected and to perform as a coach.

Opportunities to learn also are a history of accidents. For example, how one handles injuries may not be learned unless an athlete experiences a trauma that requires treatment. What kinds of changes occur in the program when a coach resigns, only are learned, if the coach leaves. How the institution, the athletic director (AD), and the coaching staff respond to the public, press, administrators, when possibly faced with a NCAA probe, due to suspected rule violations cannot be anticipated. How does one cope with athletes arrested or charged with felonies such as DWI, drug related offenses, or assault is only understood through firsthand experience.

For the apprentice evaluation is an open and continuous process. The head coach, other members of the staff, and swimmers observe and rate the performance of the apprentice. As the apprentice moves from newcomer to seasoned apprentice, others expect the mastery of skills and the understanding of nuances to improve. In the beginning, there is more leeway for error, but as experience builds the tolerance for mistakes narrows. Repeated failures may generate pressures among the coaching staff and from the athletes for dismissal. Success gains respect. It is only inside the swimming community that any recognition of the assistant's contribution to the head coach's success and to the team's performance is recognized. For people beyond the swimming community the unit of evaluation is the team. Regardless of the strategy of control used by the head coach, the head coach alone is responsible for winning and losing, not the assistants.

In short, the apprenticeship role lets the individual realistically learn the job requirements with full knowledge that if a job is well-done, acceptance is earned and entry into the coaching profession may be obtained.

The role of the assistant coach

Initially new assistants are concerned with adjusting to the program's schedule of activities. Where are facilities located, the Nautilus-type equipment, and free weights? Where is the pool? Where is the equipment stored? What are the hours for training? What kinds of equipment are needed for training sessions? When and where do athletic department meetings take place? When do coaching planning sessions occur? In the midst of this welter of activities, assistant coaches often have to adjust to their class schedules as either teachers or students or adjust to their normal work schedule if they hold another job.

How a head coach chooses to define job tasks and delegate them is an individual preference. Assistant coaches typically are responsible for providing support in handling a variety of administrative and instructional activities. In some cases, responsibilities are carefully detailed and assigned fixed for the year; in other cases, responsibilities are rotated. As the season progresses for the new assistant coach there are sets of management and technical skills which need to be mastered. The bundle of activities that have to be performed by either the head coach or one or more of the assistants (either volunteer or paid) include the tasks described in the following sections.

<u>Administrative tasks</u>.-Prior to the arrival of athletes on campus the assistant coach or the head coach must check with the academic advisor to ensure that each athlete has properly filed admission applications, sent in high school transcripts, SAT and/or ACT scores, has proof of compliance with Proposition #48,[1] has been admitted, signed contracts for housing and received room assignments, signed meal contracts, filed for insurance, and pre-registered for classes.

When swimmers arrive on campus, an assistant coach should check the class schedules to ensure there is no conflict between practice sessions and lecture/laboratory sessions. The assistant coach should act as a resource person in directing students to appropriate buildings, offices, departments, and services during the first week of adjustment on campus. The assistant coach should learn where the administrative offices are located and which officials will expedite the handling of requests.

At the beginning of the school year an assistant may arrange for appointments with the team physician to get physical examinations and drug tests.

The assistant coaches, head coach, and athletes must attend the orientation meeting during which the athletic director or the college's or university's faculty representative to the NCAA explain the NCAA rules and regulations governing conduct and eligibility of athletes. The assistant coach helps to make sure that the appropriate affidavits are signed by each athlete (each member of the coaching staff also signs) confirming their understanding of and compliance with the institution's, the conference's, and the NCAA's rules.

During the year the assistant coach is expected to attend departmental and program staff meetings as well as all required social functions. For instance, one should attend adult and student booster club functions and when appropriate, represent the athletic department at fund raising activities.

The assistant coach is responsible for the coordination of transportation of the team to departmental and school-wide functions.

At the end of the quarter or semester each athlete's transcript is reviewed by the assistant coach in order to determine academic eligibility under conference and NCAA rules. Even if there is an academic advisor, the coaching staff should check the status of each member of the team. This action facilitates getting to know the athletes' capabilities beyond simply swimming as well as sensitizing the staff to potential problems. Where problems occur the assistant coach should notify the head coach, the athletic director, and the academic counselor. Around mid-quarter or mid-semester in some schools the athletic department or coach sends a form to each of the athlete's professors. The form is a status report requesting information on class attendance and grades to date. It also asks whether the faculty member has observed any learning problems. In cases where academic troubles or potential learning disabilities are noted, the athlete is referred to the academic advisor.

At the beginning of each season and periodically throughout the season the assistant coach may be asked to purchase equipment as needed. Replacement items usually include goggles, bathing caps, drag suits, paddles, kickboards, swim fins, surgical tubing, swimsuits for practice and for competition, team T-shirts, towels, clipboards, stop watches, eyedrops, eardrops, vitamins, and various office supplies. Procedures for filing vouchers vary by institution. The assistant coach is expected to learn these procedures. To do so, the assistant coach should check with the individual on the athletic department staff who is in charge of financial matters. Once procedures have been explained, the assistant coach must adhere to them. Failure to do so may prove expensive.

Large equipment purchases may include items such as swim benches, free weights, automatic timing system, electronic scoreboard, videotaping equipment, or computer equipment, programs, and supplies. The assistant coach should work with the head coach in setting up priorities for possible fund raising projects. Once priorities have been set, the head coach or assistant can work with the fund raisers and booster club to obtain funds for their purchase.

Equipment that is assigned to each swimmer and diver must logged and records kept on equipment lost or stolen. In the event that equipment is stolen, appropriate reports must be filed with the coach, athletic director, building officials, and campus security.

An inventory of all supplies and equipment usually is taken at the end of the season or academic year. Supplies and equipment are stored when not in use.

The assistant coach or the head coach is expected to coordinate and supervise activities of the managers. Managers are to make sure all suits, sweatsuits (practice and competition), and towels, are washed. They also see that the equipment is set up for practice sessions and properly stored after each session.

Supervisory tasks.-Before the assistant coach starts working on-deck, the head coach usually explains the sequence of training for the season during various phases of the season--pre-season, mid-season and dual meet competition, and taper and championships. The coach typically covers what the sequence of training is on a weekly basis; how the dryland exercises, weights, and swimming phases of the program are integrated; and how much emphasis is given to each on a day by day basis. The organization of a typical swim practice also is discussed.

Coaches are responsible for developing various regimens for Nautilus and free weight training and for supervising each practice session. During the season for each practice, whether Nautilus or free weights, attendance is logged. Each swimmer usually is given a sheet to record performances for the session. Records should be collected by the assistants, and reviewed with comments affixed on progress, areas of weakness, strength, and activities for swimmers to target for improvement in the next session.

Assistants also are responsible for supervising dryland exercises such as aerobics, calisthenics, stretching, and running (or other activities such as bicycling, tennis, or basketball during the early pre- or post-season). In the event of an accident, the assistants should know the appropriate procedures for contacting training staff, physician, or hospital depending on the severity of the injury. The assistants should inform the head coach, and the AD if necessary. The assistants need to fill out the accident report, file insurance forms, and take care of monitoring the athlete's visits to the physician or trainer during rehabilitation. Following any injuries the assistant coaches and the head coach should be

23

informed by the physician or trainer on what modifications in training must be made.

   On-deck tasks.- On-deck coaching usually involves taking responsibility for a particular swim practice (early morning or afternoon session), or a particular set of swimmers on the team, or a particular set of lanes. Assistants either write the workouts or supervise the workout prepared by the head coach. The assistants are responsible for analysis and feedback on stroke and turn mechanics. In order to be effective eventually as an on deck coach, the apprentice needs to develop a "photographic eye." Anyone who teaches or coaches swimming should understand stroke mechanics and body movement. The coach should be able to take a mental snapshot of any phase of stroke execution, analyze that image, and identify which elements of the stroke are incorrect. Each phase of stroke execution has a particular set of visible cues to which the apprentice needs to become sensitized. The apprentice must then be able to convey a verbal image, perhaps reinforced with gestures, which communicates to the swimmer where the mistake occurs and how best to rectify it. Coaches who have developed this talent are seen by swimmers and others coaches as "good stroke technicians."

   Coaches also must learn to evaluate the relative efforts of swimmers in various strokes and distances as well as an appreciation of the intricacies of pace work. They should offer encouragement for solid performances, but not be excessively lavish in their praise. There is a delicate balance between too much criticism and too little praise, and vice versa. Too much criticism turns people off. Criticism becomes interpreted as an ad hominem attack. Whatever praise is later offered is dismissed. Similarly too much praise undermines the veracity of critique. Swimmers generally know whether they have performed maximally or at the expected levels. Too much praise for sub-par performance suggests the coach has misread the situation, and weakens the coach's reputation as knowledgeable. The coach should be sensitive to the physical and emotional states of the athlete and be able to respond appropriately.

   Assistants often gravitate to their strengths. For example, if the assistant has a solid background in aerobics or weights, then that activity tends to be favored when permitted the choice of assignments.

Assistants should be able to videotape from on-deck and from underwater observation ports the practices and competition sessions. They must learn to analyze performances and suggest ways to improve mechanics. If a film or videotape library is available, an assistant may be responsible for ordering new materials and cataloging films and cassettes.

During swim practices assistants or managers may be expected to record splits (the time required to swim a sub-set of distance for a fixed amount of yardage-- 50s within a 100, 100s within a 500 or 1000). In some programs these splits are recorded for every swimmer for each practice session. In other programs these splits are only recorded for practice sets during a given practice session or during a meet.

Both assistant coaches and swimmers should maintain a log of each practice. The log should include: what sets were swum (strokes or combinations of strokes and the yardages of each) and what time constraints were specified (time intervals for send-offs, time intervals to achieve) for fixed distances. Assistant coaches may be asked to analyze each workout in order to determine the percentage of time for aerobic and anaerobic training. They must record observations on the ease or difficulty of sets, the efficacy of particular drills, and the reactions of swimmers to sets as well as their performances.

During the competition phase of the season, one of the assistants usually is responsible for making travel reservations for the coaching staff and team. This responsibility includes: arranging hotel or motel rooms (remaining within the NCAA guidelines for the number of occupants per room and making sure to obtain the reduced rate for athletic teams and the free room for the head coach and/or bus driver); arranging for buffets and arranging for tours where possible; and arranging for transportation (vans, bus, or airlines and limousines as necessary). Arrangements should include: filing the required budget requests; obtaining travel advances from the treasurer's office; and clearing the itinerary with the head coach and the athletic director. Upon return from the trip all receipts, bills, and vouchers should be filed. The head coach over time should build a file of hotels/motels used, the prices charged, costs for buffets, phone numbers, and names of managers to contact in each of the various locales where the team regularly competes. This file speeds the process of fixing travel plans and makes the preparation of itineraries much easier.

During the competition phase of the season, an assistant makes sure to obtain meet results from coaches or sports information directors (SIDs) of schools in the conference or schools with whom meets are scheduled. Assistant coaches may be asked to prepare analyses of the opponent's team by looking at swimmer's performances in the events in which they have competed. As part of the exercise the assistant coaches should prepare a hypothetical lineup of swimmers by event to see how the team will best match up against the opponent's "best" lineup. The head coach and staff then evaluate the various lineups suggested to determine which strategy is best. If the team anticipates participating in invitational and national championships, then results from other programs expected to compete should also be obtained and studied.

During the competition phase of the season, an assistant coach usually confirms arrangements for meet schedules with visiting coaches. A copy of the itinerary, desired schedule for use of pool facilities, lodging plans, and the travel schedule are obtained. The head coaches confer in order to agree on which list of events is be swum. Any changes in eligibility of athletes are noted. Coaches confirm whether "no shave,"[2] "no Lycra" (competition suit),[3] and/or "no rest and/or taper"[4] agreements are still in effect. Assistants make any arrangements needed to ensure that the visiting coach and team are treated cordially, provided with towels, supplied with parking permits, and accommodated requests made by the visiting team's head coach.

One assistant coach usually is assigned to organize dual meets: schedules pool use; contacts the student booster organization and any other individuals who usually assist with meets telling them of the meet date and time to appear for pre-meet instructions; helps set up seating; prepares the scorer's table and diving table by laying out tablets, forms, and pencils; prepares clipboards with time cards and pencils for timers; assigns watches to timers (keeping a log of which watch is assigned to a timer); sets up electronic timing system (having starting pistols as backup for the start and the recall judge in the event of a false start); installs the touch pads and double checks the sound equipment; organizes meet officials; arranges for trainers and/or medical personnel to be on call; puts out lap counters; provides event entry cards for swimming and diving for each coach; checks on lane assignments with the visiting coach; allocates towels to the team managers to be returned after the meet; informs the media of the meet; contacts campus security to arrange for security on the parking lot and at the pool; and hangs the team banner.[5]

Prior to the conference championship meet at the end of the season the head coach and the assistant coaches verify that entries are properly completed and filed. Following the conference championship meet an assistant coach obtains certificates of Proof of Performance for NCAA, verifies that these have been filled out or properly requested, and files them with the proper NCAA meet officials.

Following the completion of events each evening at the NCAA Championship meet, should swimmers place in the consolation or finals the assistant coach verifies the scores and obtains Certificates of Participation. When swimmers place in the consolations and finals, NCAA Honorable-Mention All-American or All-American certificates are picked up. After the season the assistant coach should make sure that these certificates are "plaqued" and displayed either at the pool, the athletic department, or coach's office. Certificates of Participation are given to swimmers who participated in the NCAA meet. An assistant coach also files forms for Academic All-American when swimmers or divers are eligible. For graduating seniors who achieved Academic All-American and intend to matriculate in graduate school, application for NCAA scholarships should be submitted.

Head coach and assistant coach interaction

The head coach should recognize that volunteers and assistant coaches are serving as "apprentices." The head coach may inform the newcomers of the kinds of stroke mechanics that are desired in the program. The head coach should pass on any verbal or physical cues that assist the swimmers in focusing on stroke mechanics and correcting typical errors. The head coach needs to indicate whether stroke mechanics are to be taught using a part-progression strategy or a holistic approach.

Assistants without a coaching background in swimming pose a challenge. Lacking an experiential base, they sometimes presume that by reading voraciously the void will be filled. Appealing to the authority of the written word is a simple strategy learned from long years in school. There is a tendency for some new assistants to follow such a strategy.

Standard sources on swimming techniques and on the principles of training that are often recommended include James E. Counsilman (1977) Competitive Swimming Manual, Ernest W. Maglischo (1982) Swimming Faster, Don Gambril and Alfred Bay (1984) Swimmer and Team, Randy Reese(c 1985) Building a Championship Season with Randy Reese, and John Troup and Randy Reese (1983) A Scientific Approach to the Sport of Swimming. In addition to these texts the beginning coach should stay current with articles which are published in Swimming World and Junior Swimmer, Swimming Technique, The Journal of Swimming Research, World Clinic Year Books, and ASCA Newsletter. (Those coaches with responsibilities for working with instructional and competitive programs within the community and interested in working with Masters swimmers should look up past issues of Swim Swim, stay current with times and news in MACA Newsletter, Swim Master, and read Swim Magazine. For a brief overview of Masters swimming see Hastings (1983) or Meyer (1982) and consult the column entitled "Masters Corner" that appears fairly regularly in Swimming World and Junior Swimmer.)

As assistant coaches become experienced, they tend to de-emphasize their dependence on written materials, and move toward a reliance on teaching techniques and training hints used by other coaches. Or, they simply may rely on what best works for them. The head coach should encourage the assistant coaches to resist forsaking the professional literature. Professional journals, issues of NCAA News, announcements from FINA or U.S. Swimming that cross the desk of the head coach should automatically be routed to the assistants to read, analyze, and critique. Where funds are available, assistants should be encouraged to attend World Clinics, and ASCA clinics and workshops. If the coaching staff has too many assistants, making travel and registration costs prohibitive, then perhaps individual staff might be sent on a rotational basis of one a year. When the assistant returns from such sessions a presentation of newly learned materials should be made to the coaching staff and team. If the head coach gives clinics, new assistants should be encouraged to attend and older assistants should be asked to serve as demonstrators and co-presenters. Any chance to broaden the technical and theoretical base of knowledge of the coaching staff should be seized.

For those individuals who are new to the program there is a great deal of anxiety over what is expected of them and of making mistakes. The head coach should take steps to reduce anxiety among staff members. By carefully detailing the activities and responsibilities expected of each individual, the head coach reduces the level of anxiety among newcomers. The unknown becomes known, and thus capable of being accomplished. Structuring tasks reduces the likelihood of error. The head coach must allow the newcomer to make mistakes. Reducing the stress associated with learning a new role minimizes role distance between head coach and assistants.

Despite what is commonly believed, assistants with a swimming background do not always make good coaches. Swimmers engaged in training very often are involved in a program where the coach is concerned with controlling the actions of the individual. In such cases the swimmer seldom develops a reflective and critical appreciation of the process. Usually individuals who come from a program emphasizing dependency on the coach often can faithfully reproduce activities and drills, but fail to understand the principles upon which they are constructed. Conversely, individuals who come from a program that emphasizes reflection and an active participation in the planning and organization of training often will better understand the rationale for doing certain types of sets and drills.

After an assistant has demonstrated a commitment to learning, to coaching, and to professionalism as well as having proved one's loyalty, the coach should be willing to accept the assistant as a colleague. The head coach, when needed, should serve as an advocate for the individual. Being a colleague and an advocate include such actions as assisting in job placement, maintaining professional exchanges of information over the years, undertaking collaborative research projects or co-assignments in coaching.

The coach needs to ensure that channels of communication are always open with the rest of the coaching staff. Where questions arise concerning techniques, training sessions, issues of philosophy, role responsibilities, or ways to handle interpersonal squabbles, there must be an opportunity to answer them. Differences of opinion should be aired, noted, and resolutions negotiated when possible. Where differences persist, the head coach and assistant coaches must agree to disagree. When addressing the team the coaching staff must give the appearance of a united front. Differences of opinion between coaches always must remain among themselves, private from the athletes. Keeping coaches' opinions private reduces the possibility of conflicts becoming public and prevents swimmers from taking sides in any conflict. Individuals without experience tend to be more likely to reveal coaches' secrets to the athletes than do experienced personnel. Assistant coaches should avoid this pitfall for a team that is overly concerned with micro-politics is distracted from training, from achieving individual and team goals, and from optimal swimming performances.

Coach's assumptions in adding staff

Although the prerogative of hiring the head coach rests with the AD, the addition of volunteer coaches and hiring of assistant coaches are the duties of the head coach. The same job markers that describe the categories of experience for the head coach pertain to the assistant coaching staff. (For a discussion of head coach's job markers see Chapter 3.) The levels of excellence and experience desired vary by program.

Volunteer coaches.-Volunteer coaches usually are individuals interested in the sport either as former participants, devotees, parents with children who swim, or students fulfilling some field placement requirement in education or physical education. Volunteer coaches more often than not tend to be part-time workers. Their involvement is circumscribed by responsibilities defined elsewhere.

To recruit volunteer coaches the head coach can use a network of contacts in the local community. The head coach might contact local U.S. Swimming clubs, high schools, YMCAs, Masters programs, or individuals with aquatics backgrounds--such as alumni who swam--in order to spread the word that a job position is open. The head coach also may contact representatives in the physical education department or place an advertisement in the school paper (Leonard 1980).

Coaches, when evaluating volunteers who are interested in working with the program, need to assess the nature of their swimming background. Typical questions are: When did they swim? Where did they swim? Who was their coach? What strokes did they swim? Have they coached before? When, where, and with whom did they coach or were they on their own? Are they ASCA certified?

30

How individuals respond to these questions establish the currency of their knowledge on the state of the arts in swim mechanics, turns, starts; their level of understanding of physiology and principles underpinning training techniques; their level of competition; and their degree of familiarity with the routines and pressures confronting the coach, staff and swimmers during the season. These responses quickly allow the head coach to determine whether individual is able to work with the program. If the head coach decides to add the individual to the staff, the nature of the applicant's responses provides a clue on how much instruction will be needed, how many responsibilities may be delegated, and how much autonomy may be granted to the individual.

The head coach usually establishes what the duties of the volunteer coach are and what kind of time commitment is required. Rewards for working as a volunteer coach usually are non-monetary. Volunteer coaches may be viewed by head coaches with a degree of ambivalence. Any assistance that is competent and reliable is welcomed, especially if it is free. If the assistance is incompetent, unreliable, and unpredictable, generally any gains tend to be offset by energies expended in troubleshooting.[6] Some coaches feel that new personnel are needed to re-invigorate the program with new ideas. Other coaches feel that volunteers are unreliable and are not worth the trouble. These coaches argue that individuals are more dependable if they are under contract.

In programs with limited financial resources and without an extensive system of organizational support-- such as alumni swimmers, boosters, interested parents, and volunteer officials--very often volunteer coaches play an important role in taking care of equipment, running meets, and serving as information gatherers or administrative assistants.

Volunteer coaches generally hold the same beliefs about sports that paid coaches espouse (Gould and Martens 1979). Volunteer coaches see sports as fun and the participants' well-being as important. They see sports as promoting physical fitness. They do not see participants as spending too much time with the sport, as being under too much physical stress, or as psychologically damaged by losing. Volunteer coaches also see parents as sources of interference and complain of poor officiating. Given the fact volunteer coaches espouse similar beliefs about sport as head coaches, and willingly undertake a variety of tasks, often with a minimum of griping, it is easy for the head coach to take them for granted and sometimes unduly exploit them. The head coach needs to be sure to recognize the contribution of the volunteer staff in order to maintain equanimity between volunteers, head coach, and staff. Failure to be sensitive to the needs of volunteers may engender ill-will, conflict, or lead to individuals quitting.

Volunteer assistants often have a high rate of turnover. Graduation takes a toll. Many become disillusioned with the job. They find the hours long and the rewards minimal. They see themselves as having little impact on the program. They sometimes claim that the swimmers view them as something to be tolerated and often incompetent. Many find the pressures of work, family, and other organizational work more demanding, and time consuming, if not more interesting. They do not see coaching as a viable career option.

Other volunteers are not willing to wait and serve. As soon as they have mastered a set of activities, they feel entitled to be elevated in status or paid as an assistant. If these conditions are not met, they may tend to look elsewhere for employment or lose interest.

Paid assistants.-The same job markers apply for assistant coaches as head coaches. Assistant coaches typically fall into one of two categories: (1) full-time paid and (2) part-time paid. Full-time paid assistants fall under federal Affirmative Action requirements and the same screening measures are followed in hiring for these positions as for the head coach. Part-time paid positions do not fall under the federal employment guidelines. Universities and colleges vary on the degree of rigor expected in complying with Affirmative Action guidelines. If a job vacancy occurs at a critical point in the season, conformity to the letter of the law is less likely to be pressed than if the opening occurs during the off-season when recruiting is completed.

How much an assistant coach should be paid varies depending on the philosophy of the head coach and available budget. Some coaches believe assistants should pay the head coach for the opportunity to serve an apprenticeship with them. After all, the knowledge gleaned, the prestige acquired from working with a "top coach," and the better job possibilities following such an association justify the expense. Others believe that assistants should be paid a decent salary commensurate with the services rendered. Unfortunately swim coaches are paid little for long hours of work. Frequently a coach has to supplement a salary with another job in order to survive. Assistant coaches usually are paid even less. Often assistants who need money to survive find themselves torn between a highly paid non-coaching job and a more enjoyable low paying coaching job. Assistants forced to make a choice between enjoyment and money usually will opt for money. It is easy to understand why some head coaches believe that assistants who do not receive adequate wages are viewed as less likely to be loyal than the better paid.

1. Full-time assistant coaches.-Job applicants usually are recruited and hired with some degree of permanency assumed. In recruiting assistant coaches, the head coach relies on the network of contacts developed in the larger swimming community. In addition to personally contacting other coaches and members of the swimming community, job advertisements may be placed in the NCAA News, Chronicle of Higher Education, Swimming World and Junior Swimmer, and ASCA Employment Newsletter.

Applicants usually submit resumes in response to the advertisements. Some coaches will hire an applicant sight unseen, relying only on the cover letter, resume, and a phone call. Such an action is understandable if an assistant coach is needed immediately. Hiring someone without a personal interview is a practice to be avoided (Gambril 1983: 169-176). More often than not, the assistant will have to be replaced. Sometimes the assistant coaches are full-time graduate assistants. In such cases the head coach can release them from coaching duties, but usually they have the right to continue the scholarship until the end of the quarter or semester. This situation is an unnecessary drain of financial resources, is difficult to justify when collegiate budgets are tight, and is a waste of personnel. The interview is critical in assessing the applicant's motives in applying for the position as well as assessing whether the applicant and the head coach agree concerning the program's philosophy.

Some head coaches will not hire individuals as assistant coaches unless they claim that they eventually want to become a head coach. The head coach believes that individuals who have this goal are more willing to explore a variety of activities during their apprenticeship than individuals who want to remain as assistants. This practice probably leads to head coaches surrounding themselves with people who share similar beliefs and personality traits. If personality types in fact do evolve in a profession, selectivity in hiring practices may be a contributing factor.

Some assistant coaches may remain in a program as long as the head coach that hired them stays, or until the head coach and staff are fired. There are some fine full-time assistants who spend their entire career with one program. Others move to another position after gaining experience. Still others simply drop out of coaching.

2. Part-time paid assistants.-The head coach often employs athletes who have completed eligibility, but need financial support to finish requirements for an undergraduate degree. In many cases, these positions involve graduate stipends provided by the athletic program or the department of physical education which permit individuals to pursue a graduate degree with coaching as the stipulated condition of employment. Such positions usually are for a term of two years. Graduate assistants rarely are hired after their term of employment is completed.

Motives for remaining as an assistant coach in part depend on how the position of assistant coach is perceived by the individual and by others. For instance, how much responsibility is assigned and how much latitude one has in contributing to the over all development of the program often are factors considered when it comes time to move. The professional stature of the coach and the reputation of the program are factors also weighed in the decision making process. Finally, the calibre of competition in the conference and the reputation of the institution must be considered.

Summary

--People enter coaching for a combination of structural and personal motives. Those who enter for structural reasons do not tend to remain in coaching as long as those who entered for personal reasons.

--Before achieving the position of a head coach the individual must serve an apprenticeship as an assistant coach. One may serve as a volunteer or a paid assistant (either full-time or part-time).

--The role of the assistant coach involves learning a variety of administrative, supervisory, and on-deck tasks. The apprentice learns these tasks by watching, reading, and doing. How much instruction is provided by the head coach depends on the individual's philosophy.

--The role of the assistant coach is complex. It takes time to learn, involves long hours, has low pay, and little prestige.

--The turnover among assistant coaches is high, but those who survive often move on to become head coaches.

REVIEW QUESTIONS

1. What are the kinds of motives that lead a person into coaching? Why do you want to coach? Do you see coaching as the only career that you will have? If not, what steps have you taken to prepare for an alternative career?

2. Describe what kinds of learning opportunities are available to an individual while serving as an apprentice. Would you want a great deal of direction and instruction as an apprentice or would you prefer to be left on your own to pick up things?

3. What are the areas of activity for which an assistant coach may be responsible? Which activities would you want to learn first? Which ones would you save to learn later?

4. What are the advantages and disadvantages of serving as a volunteer coach? As a paid assistant coach?

NOTES

1   "Proposition 48 requires a 2.00 grade-point average (based on a 4.00 maximum) in a core curriculum of at least 11 academic courses including at least three years in English, two years in mathematics, two years in social science, and two years in natural science or physical science. It also requires a minimum 700 combined score on the SAT verbal and math sections or a minimum 15 composite score on the ACT." (Martin Gehring/News-Sentinel staff. No date.)   The requirements for instructional elements in each of the core courses are specified as is an indexing system to be used to phase in the application of the rule.

2   In the late 1950s swimmers discovered that removal of hair from the arms, legs, and torso reduced a feeling of drag and heightened a kinesthetic feel for the water. Swimmers when shaved generally swim faster than when unshaved. Whether this fact is best explained by principles of hydrodynamics or principles of psychology has yet to be clearly established. Incidentally, some swim coaches believe that track athletes may soon copy this practice.

3   Swimmers generally have two types of swimsuits: one is a practice suit, made of cotton, loose fitting and absorbent, creating resistance;   the other is a competition suit, made of water resistant material, form fitting, and lowering resistance.

4   For a discussion of the taper see Miller (1977) or Hannula (1984).

5   When an institution hosts a conference championship meet usually one or more of the assistants are involved in organizing the meet.   (For a discussion of procedures followed in hosting a conference championship meet see Hastings and Wantland 1986.)

6   Two problems frequently occur. First, assistant coaches sometimes like to date athletes. To prevent possible charges of sexual harassment or undue use of authority, in claims that have been made by students against superiors and have been sustained by the courts, it is best to effect a coaching staff policy of no dating of athletes by the coaches. Second, assistant coaches, if close to the ages of the athletes often like to mix with them socially. Fraternization may create problems in maintaining a clearly defined hierarchy of authority between coaching staff and athletes. It is a problem that must be monitored.

CHAPTER 3. HIRING THE HEAD COACH

"B... College has completed a new aquatics
facility and is looking for a new coach." (Jack)
"You know what that means. They are going to
bring in a big name and try and move into the top
ten." (Bill)
"Yes, but I'll bet that they hire Tim and just go
through the motion on a search. After all, he is
the only Olympian their school has ever
had."(Jack)

****

Vacancies may occur in the ranks of college
coaching for many reasons. Sometimes openings can be
anticipated when an individual is moving toward
retirement, or is struggling with a serious and
debilitating illness. Other times the position is
suddenly empty due to a firing or a surprise
resignation.

To hire a head coach is a fairly detailed
procedure. Once an opening occurs, the AD seeks
approval to open a search for a new coach. The AD sets
up a search committee, writes a job announcement, and
places the advertisement in the appropriate media
sources. In writing the job announcements, the AD and
members of the search committee agree on the kinds of
educational experience, the level of coaching
background, and the types of skills wanted in a job
candidate. These criteria appear in the job
description and are called job markers. Applicants who
read the advertisements must be able to interpret these
clues about the job, evaluate their own credentials,
and decide whether to apply or not. Applications are
filed. The AD and the search committee review the
files. Recommendations are requested and a "short
list" (a final pool of candidates) is designated.
Candidates are then interviewed. The exchange between
the candidate and the AD is especially crucial in
developing an understanding of the nature of the job
and its requirements. A contract is tendered,
considered by the applicant, and accepted or rejected.

In this chapter the typical list of job markers
used in advertisements is reviewed, as are the
assumptions of the search committee when evaluating a
job applicant's credentials. Also discussed are the
kinds of questions asked by the candidates of the AD or
in learning about the program.[1]

Job markers in employment advertisements

Each employment advertisement for coaches contains "job markers" or qualifications that denote a category of experience to be assessed. The evaluation is based on the applicant's record contained in a resume. For some kinds of activities or associations with particular individuals or programs a rating is imputed because an institutional socialization effect is presumed.

Job advertisements usually are placed in the <u>NCAA News</u>, <u>Chronicle of Higher Education</u>, <u>Swimming World and Junior Swimmer</u>, and <u>ASCA Employment Listing</u>.

Advertisements typically include the following job markers.

<u>B.S. or M.S. required</u>.-Usually a college degree is required as a minimum for employment as a coach; sometimes a Master's degree is desired, but only rarely is the Ph.D. preferred. Depending on the nature of the job, specialty skills may be designated. In addition to coaching, aquatics director's capabilities--the ability to administer an aquatics program, or oversee the construction of a new pool, or direct the expansion or repair of existing facilities--may be listed. If instruction is required, a list of aquatics or physical education courses may be noted. Certifications in first aid, lifesaving, water safety instruction also may be specified.

In some cases, an individual is expected to coach a second sport, or teach in an academic program. If a split appointment of professor/coach is advertised, then it is desirable for the applicant to have advanced degrees in order to establish credibility with the academic community. In the more competitive programs, ADs assume that the head coaching position is full-time, requiring specialized training and/or a physical education background. There is a reluctance to encourage positions with dual responsibilities. (This reluctance is also voiced occasionally by some academicians who believe that the role of teaching/research is a "calling" and coaching is "play.")

<u>Competitive experience preferred</u>.-ADs as well as others in sport assume that experience as a competitor in age-group, interscholastic, intercollegiate, national, international, or Olympic settings, (and more

recently, but less often as Masters) sensitizes the individual to the "world view" of swimmers and familiarizes the coach with the basics of a successful program. Ranked performances in one or more of these competitive levels are preferred over non-ranked performances. The more elite the level of performance, the better. Presumably elite performance reflects the moral fiber of the individual. After all, to become top flight requires discipline, training, self-sacrifice, dedication, and goal-oriented behavior. Having developed these character traits and having experienced the rewards they bring presumably enables one to instill them more easily in others. To date, no research exists that firmly establishes a connection between level of performance, personality traits, and leadership traits or the ability to teach.

A reputation as a successful elite swimmer allegedly confers the ability to attract the attention of "blue chip" swimmers when recruiting. Top flight athletes are presumably well-informed on the sport's history as well as its heroes and heroines. Participation is no guarantee of being well-informed. Ironically, available research suggests that name recognition of athletes or coaches tends to be generationally specific. A swimmer of earlier fame with five or ten years of coaching experience probably will not be recognized as a swimmer by the current generation of recruits. Name recognition of earlier heroes and heroines typically is limited to the history buffs.

Coaching experience preferred.-In some cases a minimum number of years of experience is specified in the advertisement. It is assumed that organizational abilities including technical, management, and communication skills were learned or sharpened, if the applicant served as an apprentice or had the sole responsibility for directing a program.

Ability to coach and compete successfully at specified divisional level.-Athletic directors generally desire an applicant who has coached at the level advertised. The coach's record is evaluated by the team's record in dual competition, conference and NCAA rankings; and the numbers of individuals qualifying for honors regionally, nationally, internationally; or the numbers of individuals qualifying as Honorable Mention, All-American Prep or High School; of the numbers of individuals who qualified as All-American College Divisions I, II, or

III; or individuals qualifying for the Olympic trials or making the Olympic team.

If an applicant has not coached at the level advertised, then the applicant should be well-known and respected among the more reputable coaches at an equal the rank of experience. Coaches apparently move within divisions more easily than across divisions. It also appears easier to move down from level I to II or III than to move up in levels.[2]

Demonstrated ability to recruit.- Applicants with experience as head coaches or assistant coaches are presumed to be knowledgeable of NCAA rules on recruiting. Recruiting success is measured by the program's performance record. Another way to evaluate recruiting success is look at the excellence of the athletes recruited judged against the academic standing of the institution. Generally it is more difficult to find large numbers of elite athletes who are also outstanding scholars.

Applications for the head coach position received by the AD usually contain a cover letter, resume, and letters of recommendation. In some cases, copies of media releases extolling the merits of the applicant's abilities as a coach, competitor, and "humanitarian" also are included. (Incidentally, an applicant may err by sending too many letters of recommendation. An administrator may ask, why the information overload? Is something wrong with this individual?)

In screening applicants not only is the "fit" between the individual's record and job description important, but so is the influence of networks. Before a candidate is invited for an interview, the AD not only contacts the applicant's references for letters of recommendation, but also any individuals with knowledge of the candidate. If the applicant does not receive a strong endorsement from "knowledgeable acquaintances" and colleagues who are part of the AD's network, the applicant usually is dropped from further consideration in the screening process.

The impressions made by the candidate during the interview are perhaps the more crucial factors in the decision to hire. Typically the applicant meets with members of the athletic department staff, head coaches, support personnel, key administrators, faculty, and athletes. In some cases, reactions from each of these parties are solicited by the AD. In other cases, only selected parties have input on the decision whether to hire or not. To establish rapport easily with individuals, to express oneself clearly and cogently without equivocation, and to present oneself as confident, knowledgeable, and organized are important traits, if the candidate expects to survive the interview process. The candidate should be able to employ the rhetoric of sport, see the position as "an opportunity for personal growth" and as a "challenge to originate a program, rebuild the program," or merely "maintain its standard of excellence." Given these traits and skills, the individual will presumably be able to administer the program, coach the athletes, work harmoniously with staff, faculty, administrators, and parents, and interact with representatives from other audiences supporting the athletic department.

Although the position of head coach falls under Affirmative Action requirements, colleges and universities vary markedly in the stringency with which these rules are enforced. Some jobs are advertised in one of the many available organs that satisfy Affirmative Action requirements for notifying the public of the job, but the ads are placed in journals, newspapers, newsletters, or magazines not normally read by a wide segment of the coaching population. Some jobs are widely advertised, conforming to the spirit of the law. Even if proper notification of the job occurs, the length of time that the job description runs varies. In some cases the job announcement will appear in a single issue; in other cases it may run a month to three months. Sometimes the closing date for applications provides sufficient leeway for open competition to occur among applicants. In other cases the closing date precludes anyone without inside knowledge from applying. Applicants know that the "openness" of the search is moot when they hear through the grapevine--the network of friends and acquaintances in the coaching profession--that the job is "locked up." If a former assistant, an alumnus of the institution, or a protege of the former coach who achieved notoriety as a competitor is in line to be hired, advertising is mere window dressing and fails to satisfy the spirit of the law.

Applicants for jobs recognize that a "good old boy" system still operates. As long as the government continues to overlook those practices that violate Affirmative Action guidelines, the opportunity for upward mobility will be severely limited. Job applicants do not like the "good old boy" system unless they are well connected and assured of being included in the final pool or being invited for an interview.

Nonetheless, the majority of the applicants believe that they must tolerate the system. If they do not and legally challenge the hiring procedures of a particular institution, they assume that their names may be spread among ADs as trouble-makers; they may be informally blacklisted.

Despite the increased numbers of females participating in sport and the increased availability of programs across sports now open to women, it is well recognized that the numbers of females in head coaching jobs have fallen and the numbers of males have risen. However, the numbers of women as assistant coaches have risen in the past few years (Holmen and Parkhouse 1981). This decline in the ranks of women head coaches is due to six factors. First, some of the loss was due to reorganization as many athletic departments moved to conform to Title IX funding requirements. Second, as women's coaching jobs were redefined under the Affirmative Action regulations as gender free and the pressures of unemployment increased, males moved into vacancies left by women leaving the profession. Third, the recruitment of females was curtailed by the operation of the good old boy network. Fourth, coaching as a career choice has not been as popular among females as among males (McElroy 1981). Fifth, some of the female coaches who left the profession claim that they entered coaching only at the request of someone else (structural motive)--they claim that coaching conflicts with other activities, or they want to do something else with their lives (Hart, Hasbrook, and Mathes 1986). Sixth, female coaches reportedly suffer higher levels of burnout than do male coaches (Caccese and Mayerberg 1984).

Candidate's questions asked of the AD

Before visiting a campus, or while on campus for the interview, the candidate should become familiar with the organizational structure of the athletic program. Listed below are key topics to probe and several kinds of questions that should be asked.

Status of the program.-Is the program expanding by adding new sports, moving into another division, or upgrading the calibre of competition? Is the program maintaining itself or experiencing reorganization and/or the financial woes of retrenchment? Is the program declining? Does the program have a "clean bill of health" in dealing with the NCAA or is there a history of violations? Are there storm clouds of forthcoming penalties with athletes being declared ineligible, restrictions in recruiting, limitations on the allowable number of scholarships, and/or the possibility of probation with restrictions on participating in championship meets or TV appearances?

Responses to these questions quickly establish whether the position is professionally challenging or simply a "caretaker's" role. Where upgrading, expansion, or reorganizing are expected in the program (perhaps to rectify procedures and operations that precipitated the wrath of watchdog agencies), the pressure to produce is increased. Where maintenance or retrenchment is being emphasized until better times, the pressures are less.

Funds.-How are the athletic department and the specific programs funded? Are the monies generated at the gate, through TV revenues, at concessions, with fund drives, or by student funds (fees)? Is it some combination of these sources? What types of fund-raising activities are permissible using the institution's facilities? Is the coach expected to run a summer program, teaching clinic, or community service programs? Do these fees accrue to the department, program, or the coach? Similarly, who bears the costs for running these activities?

Responses to these questions inform the coach on the extent of community use of the facility, whether there are instructional and competitive programs connected to the university's program and dependent on its facilities, and whether there are the opportunities for earning extra income beyond that stipulated in the contract.

How does the program's budget compare with other programs in the conference, or other programs at the same level of competitiveness? How much money is available for full-time, or part-time assistants and other staff; for travel (types of travel and costs covered by department versus out-of-pocket expenses); for recruitment; for equipment; and for miscellaneous? Is the budget balanced at the end of each calendar year or are funds carried forward to the next budgetary year? What are the constraints on direct purchasing versus bids? What kinds of bids are permissible? Is the coach responsible for fund raising for the program? Does the department have a fund raiser? Is a professional fund-raising business firm employed? Or does the institution take this responsibility?

Answers to these questions identify the overall financial structure of the program, the relative contribution of institutional and non-institutional monies, and the amount of energy to be expended in fund-raising efforts. Those head coaches who are comfortable in dealing with financial matters will be successful where a heavy involvement in the business end of the sport is expected. Those head coaches without financial acumen would do well to work with a financial consultant.

Is there parity in the number of scholarships offered in this program compared with other programs in the conference? Do out-of-state athletes on scholarship receive a waiver of out-of-state tuition and fees and receive in-state tuition and fees?

Answers to these items allow the coach to calculate how many athletes can be recruited and how dollars can be allocated to athletes for books, tuition, and/or board?

Sex-segregation.-Is the athletics department sex segregated, or integrated? If it is segregated, does the men's or the women's program control access to facilities, use of equipment, dictate available practice hours, and approve competition sites? If it is segregated, is there pressure for each program to furnish their own equipment regardless of cost, or do teams share equipment? Do teams practice together or separately? Do teams travel together and compete against the same opponents? Is interaction between men and women encouraged, discouraged, or not an issue? What is the level of mutual assistance between programs in using student booster organizations, meet officials, or cheerleaders?

If the programs are separated, responses to these questions will allow the head coach to determine the magnitude of sexual discrimination found in athletics at the institution. The coach will be better able to plan the competition schedule, arrange for pool time for practices and meets, and anticipate costs for buying new equipment or replacing old equipment. The coach will also better anticipate what kinds of organization activities will be most time consuming in preparing for meets and in hosting other program events.

Athletic program success.-What is the recognized philosophy of the program? Is the program expected to win, place, or show in the conference championship?

What is the contribution of the program to the all-sport trophy in the conference? Is the program merely expected to field a team, win occasionally, win the majority of its dual meets, or go undefeated? Is the dual meet season more important than the conference championship? Do NCAA rankings take precedence over conference rankings? Is the objective merely to provide an opportunity for learning physical skills as part of the development of the scholar-athlete, and to offer the opportunity for intercollegiate competition? Is the goal to produce elite athletes competitive nationally and internationally?

Before a candidate arrives on campus an awareness of the general reputation of the athletic department and the program is usual. The coach who is expected to do well during the dual meet season probably will schedule schools with weaker programs. This coach follows a sequence of training that emphasizes preparation for a number of dual meets during the season rather than aiming for a conference or NCAA meet. Conversely, a coach who is expected to excel in both the conference and nationally is less likely to "load" the dual meet season and more likely to emphasize the taper and going for elite performances. By selecting a particular strategy, this coach attempts to control the number of factors that affect the win-loss record. By ensuring a record that conforms to program goals, this head coach's job security and tenure are enhanced.

Academics.-What are the priorities attached to academics? Do academic issues assume priority over extracurricular activities? Do athletes receive preferential treatment as part of the admissions policy? Are quotas fixed for each sport (the admissions office ensuring that each sport receive a given number of athletes each year)? If so, which sports are given priority? If two applicants are equally qualified for admission, will the athlete be given preference over the non-athlete for admission? Does the admissions office cooperate with the athletic department in recruitment, admissions, and eligibility checks? Are standards for admission stiffer for athletes than for non-athletes? Does the admissions office notify coaches or the athletic department if an applicant has an interest in a given sport?

Responses to these questions identify the institutional boundaries within which the coach is expected to recruit. The coach should also find out which NCAA or conference rules pertain in recruiting student-athletes. Responses to these questions delineate for a candidate the expectations of the administration, athletic department, and faculty on the relationship between athletics and academics. As long as athletics are housed on university and college campuses, there will be cross-pressures. On the one hand, athletic departments will be expected to provide opportunities for participation, an exciting product to watch, and a successful program with which people can identify. On the other hand, athletic departments will be expected to place academics before athletics, eschew crass commercialism, and avoid excessive exploitation in favor of fairness in business practices (Coakley 1986).

Does the athletic program have an academic advisor? Does the athletic department have a system for providing tutors for athletes and graduate assistants working with the program? Is there a designated study hall, laboratory, or area with computers available to athletes? Are study hours required? Is there a departmental regulation on minimum required grade point average (GPA) before travel is permitted? Do athletes receive recognition for scholastic excellence? What is the team GPA? What is the team's graduation rate relative to the institutional rate or the sport-specific rate across institutions? Is there a policy requiring class attendance? Is competition scheduled during exams? If so, can exams be taken under the honor system or under the supervision of a proctor when the team travels? Does the institution have a reputation of adhering to its academic requirements when dealing with athletes or are rules bent and exceptions made?

Responses to these items provide guidelines on the scope of the coach's responsibilities in handling academic problems and coordinating with an Academic Advisor where one is available. The institution of sport is increasingly being bureaucratized and subject to legislative and judicial controls. To conform to legal rules and guidelines and to fulfill institutional obligations to the athletes, a variety of special job positions have been created. This move toward specialization tends to vary by institution, the degree of competitiveness of the programs, associational affiliation (NAIA or NCAA), and divisional level. In programs where there is a proliferation of job positions, duties formerly handled by the coach alone now get delegated. The coach increasingly is left to coach and act as an administrator. In other programs that do not add new positions, the coach increasingly assumes new duties and faces more pressure.

Coach-athlete rapport.-Is the ambience open--fostering free-flowing communication between administrators, coaches, and athletes? Is it "controlled"--making athletes highly dependent on coach and staff for scheduling of daily activities, both athletic and non-athletic? Does the program have a history of good relationships between coach and athletes? Is rapport with athletes important for job tenure? Is greater emphasis placed on winning or on maintaining harmony? If conflicts develop, will the AD side with the coach or with the athlete(s)? In matters of discontent, what criteria are used to determine whether the coach should be dismissed or that athlete(s) be released? How much latitude does the coach have in maintaining control over program content and the athletes? What kinds of procedures are followed when athletes violate the law, rules of student conduct, or athletic department or team regulations?

Any violations of the law that bring the athlete into contact with the police and the courts create problems for the athletic department staff and the coach. The image of the athletic department is instantly stigmatized by the athlete's conduct. Spokespersons for the college or university and athletic program typically move quickly to isolate the athlete from the athletic department by suspension from the particular sport program either temporarily or permanently until such time as the charges have been cleared, with guilt or innocence determined. Administrators may choose to wait until the criminal courts have decided matters or may move to separate the student from the institution using proceedings for handling violations of student conduct. This academic system of procedures is entirely separate from the criminal system and the civil system. Coaches need to be careful to act in accordance with administrative and legal procedures. Procedures vary from one institution to another and from one conference to another. Failure to stay within the guidelines may result in embarrassment, legal actions, or dismissal.

Should athletes be found in violation of student conduct codes, they may be sentenced and the institution's and athletic department's image cleaned up. Athletes also may be punished by the athletic department for violation of team or departmental rules.

Infractions of the law and codes of conduct are events not happily anticipated by coaches and athletic directors. The repercussions from such events may devastate a coach's career or may merely be seen as noxious. At the worst, coaches either may be forced to voluntarily resign or be fired when the violations are seen as offensive by the community, administrators, or the athletic department. At the very least, investigations are time consuming, enervating, and detract from the business of training, competition, and program development.

In some athletic departments the win and loss record is less important than is maintaining peaceful relations between coach and swimmers. Conflict is seen as counterproductive, for the emotional upheaval which it creates often inhibits athletes from achieving top-level performances. Traditionally disagreements between coach and athletes see ADs as aligning with the coach. Athletes are seen as more substitutable than coaches. However, should a history of stormy relationships develop, the athletic director may opt to fire the coach, or effect a clean sweep and drop the program.

The coach must have a clear understanding of how much authority one maintains in establishing program structure and controlling the athletes. Autonomy clearly focuses responsibility for decisions and actions on the coach. It also increases personal risk of job loss, if failure should occur. If the athletic director constantly monitors the decisions and actions of the coach, whether knowledgeable about the sport or not, then loss of autonomy may prove counterproductive to the growth of the program. It will certainly undermine the authority of the coach in the eyes of the staff and athletes. With the head coach's loss of authority and autonomy, responsibility spreads to both the AD and coach for program failure and reduces personal risk to the head coach of job loss. Realistically, closer monitoring usually increases the likelihood of spotting an error and affixing blame.

Community support for age-group swimming.- Is there an organizational base for age-group swimming in the community? If so, what organizations are involved? Does the YMCA have an instructional and/or competitive program? Does the college or university sponsor an instructional and/or competitive program open to the community through an extension program or continuing education program? Does a U.S. Swimming program use the pool and is it coached by the head coach? Are swimmers used as staff for the U.S. Swimming program?

Does the swim program recruit swimmers from these programs? Do age-group coaches encourage, discourage, or remain relatively neutral, when their swimmers are recruited by, visit at, or attend the institution?

Do the age-group programs contribute financially through Swimathons or fund-raising efforts to a financial pool that supports both an age-group and an intercollegiate program? Does a Masters program exist for older swimmers which is part of the same administrative and financial structure?

Responses to these questions identify for the incoming coach the nature of coaching responsibilities. If the age-group and Masters programs are part of the overall structure of the swimming program, then the head coach's responsibilities are much more complex. The administrative structure will be more elaborate. One or more assistant coaches will probably be assigned to age-groupers in U.S. Swimming and one assistant may be responsible for the Masters program. The head coach will be responsible for coordinating the action of the assistants, overseeing the schedule of pool use and training, acting as a backup in handling administrative detail in scheduling meets for age-groupers and Masters, and serving as the liaison between parents and swimmers.

If a connection exists between U.S. Swimming and Masters and the intercollegiate program, there usually is a sufficiently large number of people who can assist in organizing and running a meet, whether the meet serves youth, collegians, middle-aged, or elderly. From this pool of personnel, officials, referees, timers, computer operators, timing system operators, announcers, electricians, printers, cooks, artists, and so forth can be solicited for help in hosting various events when needed. If the program is large enough, the institution can easily host dual, regional, and national meets for age-groupers, collegians, and Masters as well as international meets. Without an available pool of supporters and officials to call on, even the hosting of a dual meet can be problematic.

If a U.S. Swimming program is affiliated with an intercollegiate program, recruitment within the region is usually easier. The coach and the staff are visible among age-groupers and parents. More likely than not, swimmers and families have visited the site and have some familiarity with facilities. If the collegiate or university program has a solid reputation, then the visibility of the coach at age-group meets serves as a vehicle for letting swimmer and coach become acquainted before the formal process of recruitment occurs during the swimmer's senior year in high school.

If there is a clinic for competitive swimmers, the head coach can staff the camp with assistant coaches or collegiate swimmers. Those swimmers who attend the clinic will have the opportunity to learn not only the techniques used by the head coach, but will build ties with the head coach, the staff, and college-level swimmers. Coaches must be careful when running clinics not to violate NCAA rules on recruiting, especially those rules dealing with class standing and visits to campus.

Summary

--Filling an opening for the position of head coach is a process of many steps.

--The AD must obtain approval to open a search for a new coach. Once approval is granted, a job announcement must be placed in the appropriate outlets. Applications are received. Files are reviewed. Networks are used to check on applicants. Candidates are interviewed. Appropriate parties on campus are consulted for advice. A contract is tendered. If accepted, a new head coach is hired.

--Applicants read job announcements or hear of it through the grapevine. They decide whether to apply depending on the nature of the job markers, their evaluation of their own credentials, and an examination of their motives. Candidates interview, look at the advantages and disadvantages of the job, and decide whether they wish to continue or withdraw from further consideration. A contract is offered. The candidate refuses or accepts.

--Both the applicant and AD decide whether to continue the dialogue or terminate it. Important to the applicant are responses to questions on: the status of the program; the availability of funds; the program's emphasis on success; the importance attached to athletics versus academics; the ambience in the athletic department; and the nature of community support for swimming. Important to the AD are the applicants credentials and personality.

REVIEW QUESTIONS

1. What are some of the sources that an individual might use when looking for a job?

2. What are the steps involved in hiring a head coach?

3. What is meant by the term job markers? On which markers are you the strongest? On which are you the weakest?

4. How important is formal education in obtaining a college coaching job? Do you need to have been a swimmer to get a job? How is one's service as an apprentice evaluated? How is one's previous coaching record evaluated?

5. What topics should you address when inquiring about an athletic program?

NOTES

1 Generally, the mobility of coaches is looked at three ways by sport sociologists. The first approach treats career mobility as a ladder with the rungs of entry, apprenticeship, assistant, and head coach. Job entry and upward mobility are seen as a product of credentials, experience, and sponsorship. The second approach sees career mobility as structured by opportunities available in the market. The market is arranged by type of program (age-groupers, high school, and collegiate). The collegiate segment of the market is divided by association and divisions. Within the collegiate market opportunities are limited to head coach and assistants. Mobility is seen as primarily dependent on experience and sponsorship and secondarily on credentials. The third approach treats job openings as vacancies and describes mobility into and out of slots as a stochastic process. Such a mathematical treatment goes well beyond the bounds of this manuscript. (For an example of this approach see Smith and Abbott 1983.)

2 Although I know of no research on this aspect of job mobility, I suspect that two factors account for the growing stratification in job opportunities. First, the move from an open system of competition among colleges and universities of all sizes to a system of divisions may have broken the earlier strangle hold of a small network of coaches trained in a few elite physical education departments. Second, the more years that the system of divisions has operated, the greater the number of assistant coaches and head coaches who apprenticed in a particular division. Thus, ADs are now able to limit their searches to individuals from a particular level of experience.

CHAPTER 4.-THE HEAD COACH'S ORGANIZATIONAL AND COMMUNICATION ROLES

"Coach, when you first started coaching didn't you think you were going to spend most of your time working with the swimmers on their stroke techniques and setting up training schedules?"
"Yes, but you quickly learn that this job has two other parts. You have to be organized and you have to be a good listener and talker."

"Kenny, you have been coaching for ten years now. What is the most difficult part of the job?"
"Like any job, if you do it long enough you establish a routine. You do things automatically. You fill out the same reports, face the same deadlines, and you hear the same problems repeated each year. It is easy to forget that the swimmers stay the same age and you are getting older. You get cynical and jaundiced unless you occasionally remind yourself that coaching is a 'people' job."
"What do you mean by that?"
"Most jobs make things or move paper in some way. A people job means you have put in a good day's work if you have talked with someone else and solved a problem or made them feel better."
"Are communication skills more important than a technical knowledge of swimming?"
"I don't know, but you better be able to get your ideas across to others."

****

The job of swimming coach encompasses a combination of social skills and personal abilities. These skills and abilities allow the coach to fulfill the various organizational responsibilities of the position as well as interact with the student-athletes.

The organizational role cluster

There are two important role clusters that are part of the bundle of roles played by the coach. The first is the organizational role cluster, which encompasses a <u>technical</u> and a <u>managerial</u> side of the job. The second important role cluster is <u>communication</u>. The communication role is one of the more complex role clusters that the coach performs.

<u>Technical dimension</u>.-According to Armistead (1980: 45-46), the technical dimension includes the following activities. (For a more detailed listing of technique-oriented topics than those identified by Armistead (1980) and topics that must eventually be learned by coaches see note 1 at the end of this chapter.)[1]

1. Training and competing.[2]-These two responsibility areas address a number of questions. For instance, who runs the workout? The head coach cannot run every workout during the year and expect to remain 100 percent effective. Morning practices may be delegated to the assistant coach. Or the assistant coaches and the head coach alternate the sessions for which each is responsible. Different faces provide variety for the swimmers. If all the coaches are responsible for morning workouts at various times during the season, it serves to reduce the social distance between swimmers and coaching staff. After all, misery loves company.

During afternoon workouts, does the head coach assign assistant coaches to groups, or lanes, or the handling of clerical tasks? Does the head coach tacitly oversee the workout or actively run the entire show?

How are swimmers to be assigned to groups? The coach has a number of options depending on how much control one wishes to exercise and how the assistant coaches' roles are defined in the program. First, the head coach can assign a group of swimmers to an assistant for the entire year. The assistant becomes responsible for working with a small and manageable group while learning the program structure as well as the personalities of the swimmers. The advantage to this approach is that the assistant serves as a conduit to the head coach for detailed information on the physical and emotional well-being of a limited number of swimmers. In staff sessions it is easy, then for the head coach to obtain feedback on the progress and status of the team from each of the assistants. The head coach can suggest strategies to cope with problems or intervene, if necessary. This approach allows the assistant to take responsibility in running all phases of the program from the beginning of the season to the end. To prevent assistants from making a mistake that would be detrimental to either the program or an individual, the coach should monitor the assistants' actions.

56

Second, if the head coach wishes to maintain control over the entire team, assistants may be assigned the more mundane tasks of information gatherers and equipment handlers. This approach creates a strong dependency between swimmers and head coach. There is no buffer when interpersonal problems arise. This approach limits the involvement of the assistants. Their role are passive, based on observation rather than doing. Many assistants who apprentice in this type of program become disillusioned and drop out, unless the coach's reputation counterbalances the frustration of the assistant playing a passive role.

Third, if the head coach wants assistants to learn all phases of the program, assignments may be rotated on a regular basis so that each phase of training responsibility is learned and working with each swimmer is experienced. This approach allows the head coach to oversee the program. It reduces the opportunity for swimmers to build dependencies with a particular assistant coach. It also reduces the likelihood that, if a particular coach and swimmer have a personality conflict, they will be forced to interact with one another over a long time.

Other issues that might be addressed include: What strokes will be practiced? What group will swim in a particular lane? Will swimmers swim one, two, or more to a lane? Will "circle" swimming be used? Will "waves" or "staggered" starts along the lanes be used? Responses to such questions usually are dictated by how many swimmers are in the program, the size of the pool, and whether the pool is set up for long course or short course. What equipment will be needed? What sets will be swum? What phases of training and/or stroke will be stressed? More often than not the time of season and how well the team has progressed to date predetermines the answers to these questions.

What items should the coaching staff stress in a given practice? Usually a coaches' meeting either at the beginning of the week or before each practice addresses the above sets of questions. Clearly these types of questions receive a lot of attention in the professional literature on coaching and consume the most time on a daily basis.

2. Running meets.-The proper execution of meets receives some discussion in the literature, but by and large this skill is learned as an apprentice or while serving a stint as a head coach (see Chapter 2).

3. Recruiting.-This area of responsibility involves the administration and conduct of the process of recruiting. The tasks are "scouting, contacting, rule observance and communication" (Armistead 1980: 45). (For more detail see Chapter 6.)

4. Public relations and promotions.-These two responsibilities involve the creation of support for competitive swimming in the community served by the program as well as the building a loyal audience. Typically, two kinds of skills are needed. First is the ability to plan and execute promotional activities in cooperation with representatives from the sports information office as well as with various media people. Second is the ability to develop a social and financial system of support through adult and student booster organizations as well as other campus and community organizations (see Chapter 6).

Managerial dimension.-Again, following Armistead the managerial dimension of the job includes the activities discussed in the sections below.

1. Administering current or prospective personnel.-Styles of control and philosophy of management are discussed later in this chapter. These tasks include hiring and firing of staff when necessary (see Chapter 2).

2. Planning and organizing of the program agenda.-These topics include the following tasks. The first task is the scheduling of meets--such as NCAA Championships, Conference championships, dual meets, and special meets--and the writing of contracts between schools for dual meets. The matter of scheduling is usually left to the head coach but may be subject to the approval of the AD. Often, juggling of the schedule from year to year is necessary to balance away and home meets to limit the number of long distance trips (excellent enticements for recruiting, but expensive), and to ensure the proper mix of opponents (conference and non-conference, or easy versus hard).

Second is the scheduling and integrating of practices--swimming, dryland exercises, aerobics, calisthenics, and weights (see Chapter 2).

Third is scheduling, attending, and overseeing (where appropriate) meetings with coaching staff, with the team, and with individuals for conferences; with people from the athletic department; with key people inside the sports community; and with other people outside the sports community.

3. Handling the budget.-The head coach estimates the costs of personnel. It is important to be sure to include salary increases in the budget projection. If the head coach fails to include them in the projected total, if any cuts are effected, then someone may miss out on a raise.

The head coach also estimates the costs for new equipment or replacements. For regular and relatively inexpensive equipment purchases, the budget usually has sufficient funds. For larger and expensive equipment purchases, the head coach needs to work with the AD, the fund-raising or development officer, and the boosters. It is important to try and obtain sponsorship from vested individuals and corporate interests in the community.

Costs of transportation, lodging, and food for travel to meets or when training at home during vacation breaks must be projected. The head coach needs to talk to other coaches in the department to find out how to estimate costs for various trips. Usually the various sports teams within a department will compete against the same schools. If the school is a member of a conference, then it is expected that members compete against other in the various sports. Similarly, most sports in an athletic department usually compete against other teams at roughly the same level of competition.

The head coach needs to plan for costs of recruitment. Depending on what kind of recruiting practices are permitted and the status and stage of development of the program, costs for recruiting will vary markedly (see Chapter 6).

Operating costs--expenses for pool rental, running of meetings, officials, organizational dues, telephone, and stationery usually are covered as part of the budget. Sometimes items are covered by the athletic department, sometimes by the swimming program. It is important to figure exactly where program funds are required. This information usually can be obtained from the secretarial staff member in charge of finances.

Finally, the head coach must identify the sources of income from the college or university budget, from development funds, and special projects. The head coach usually discusses the budget with the AD. It is important to ascertain whether (1) increased funding will be available, (2) a zero-based budget will be in effect, or (3) retrenchment is to be expected. The appropriate procedures for the completion and submission of forms can be learned by working with the appropriate person on the athletic department secretarial staff in charge of money matters.

4. Overseeing the clerical work.-The head coach is responsible for oversight and double checking of details on paper-work associated with each of the above areas as necessary. Two sets of activities are involved. The first task is the coordination of the correspondence and the flow of administrative information and paper work handled by the secretarial staff. The second task is the control of the record keeping and data entry tasks assigned to assistant coaches, managers, and work study students.

The communication role cluster

The second important role cluster is communication. The role of communicator is one of the more complex role clusters that the coach performs.

Styles of communication.-Behavioral scientists who study the process of communication define it as the exchange of information between people through the sending and receiving of messages. Messages include two parts: verbal and non-verbal. A number of coding schemes have been developed by social psychologists and sociologists over the years to analyze what people say to one another. Verbal statements are counted to see who talks the most or the least. Statements are coded for who is sending the message as well as who is receiving it. This identifies flows of conversation between individuals. Verbal statements also are coded and sorted according to the content of the messages. Robert Bales and his colleagues developed a technique called interaction process analysis to examine verbal statements in groups. Bales (1966) identifies three types of verbal behavior: (1) activity statements made by the individual to be different from others and achieve personal goals; (2) task ability statements aimed at achieving group goals; and (3) likability statements offered to set up and maintain social ties between individuals. What people repeatedly emphasize in conversation is recognized by others. Sometimes it is called style. Other times it is simply assumed to be part of an individual's personality.

For instance, individuals who tend to overwhelm others in sheer volume of conversation are displaying a form of "dominance" behavior. Such behavior quickly makes one known to others, although there is no guarantee that the speaker will be liked by the listeners. Individuals who tend to focus on task completion are "problem solvers, instrumental leaders, or task specialists." These are the people who say: "let's get down to business," "let's get on with it," and "stop fooling around and let's get busy." Individuals who tend to be concerned with emotive behavior are seen as "socio-emotional leaders." Individuals who are identified as effective leaders in groups tend to mix each of these styles over time when interacting with others.

Other schemes have been used with different categories to examine styles of communication between teachers and students in physical activity. Anderson and Barrette (1978) studied the behavior of physical education teachers instructing in the gym and found that they were busy communicators, moving among students and holding conversations lasting from a few seconds to several minutes. Much of their behavior emphasized observation, provision of instruction, and organization. Cheffers and Mancini (1978) found that physical education teachers spend a disproportionate amount of time giving information, directions, and offering criticism, and lower amounts of time giving praise or showing acceptance.

Settings.-The pool also is a setting in which training and teaching are expected. The coach, like the physical educator, is expected to operate in an information dispensing mode--most messages deal with giving of information, giving directions, offering criticisms, and sometimes offering praise. While on-deck the coach tends to be autocratic, foreclosing free-wheeling conversation. The flow of conversation moves from the head coach to the assistant coaches and then to the swimmers, or directly from the head coach to the swimmers. The same pattern noted for physical education teachers is seen in swim practices. Communications are directed to every athlete. The conversations tend to be too short, limited to the rest intervals between swimming (work) sets. Note that differences usually exist in the volume and intensity of interaction between early morning practices and afternoon practices. The morning practices are marked by a smaller volume of verbal communication; afternoon sessions have a larger volume. Swimmers tend to ask questions for clarification of instructions and seek acceptance or praise. If questions are not answered, swimmers expresses feelings of confusion and frustration, and eventually lapse into silence. Studies of athletes show that they expect coaches to act as critic and instructor during practices (Fisher et al. 1982: 388-404). In fact, if the head coach does not act as a critical observer, offering criticisms and suggestions, the swimmers begin to question whether the coach is acting in a professional manner. Observation without comment is interpreted as poor job performance.

Over time, as the experience of the teacher or coach increases, there is more emphasis on sending instructional messages to the student or athletes; more feedback also is offered. With experience, feedback moves from criticism only, to a positive reinforcement mode. Coaches learn to recognize that even constructive criticism, when repeated often, eventually gets interpreted negatively. Criticism that is a mix of a positive statement plus a corrective comment is more palatable to the athlete. Not only is the coach more effective in eliciting the desired behavior when he/she uses this style of communication, but the swimmer expresses positive sentiments toward the coach for using the style over the more typical pattern of giving directions, explaining, and informing (Rushall and Smith 1979: 138-150).[3]

A persistent complaint by athletes about their coaches is that coaches tend to be activity-oriented in their patterns of communication and to deemphasize likability patterns of communication. As already noted, research does show that coaches stress direction, instruction, and criticism. Even if the coach modifies personal behavior and uses a style of instruction that combines positive reinforcement with constructive criticism, the athletes still voice the same complaint. Perhaps a pattern of "relative deprivation" exists among college or university swimmers, especially freshmen. As age-groupers, they probably received more praise and personal attention than they do as collegiate swimmers. The swimmers use the behavior of their age-group coaches as a criterion to judge the actions of their college coach. By comparison, it may very well be that the collegiate coach spends less time with each swimmer and does offer less praise. It is also possible that as an age-grouper, the athlete was the best or among the best on the team, but as a collegiate swimmer is average or just another member of the team. Falling from a position of stardom to merely being one of the team (status drop) is a difficult adjustment. Accompanying a status drop is a reduction in the level of praise to which one formerly was accustomed.

The collegiate coach may make a concerted effort to pay more attention to the swimmers. The coach using his/her own past behavior as a bench mark sees the increased expenditure of effort as an improvement. The swimmers still see the coach's style of behavior as relatively non-supportive. The problem is the swimmers are making a judgment using another coach's behavior as the criterion rather than the past behaviors of the current coach. If the collegiate coach's efforts continually fall short and are criticized regardless of efforts made by the coach to change, then the coach tends to become disenchanted, if not cynical, about any possible gains obtained from such an effort. The coach sees himself/herself as positive, open, and a good communicator. The swimmers see the coach as less than ideal. The repetition of the same complaint over the years eventually gets dismissed. The coach claims no matter what you do to try and be open and supportive, it is never enough. The coach sees the swimmers as a bottomless pit into which praise can be poured endlessly. Eventually the coach stops trying.

As the skill level or mastery of subject matter increases in the teacher or coach, the messages tend increasingly to emphasize demonstration. There is more emphasis on teaching and giving of directions.

If the coach only communicates with the swimmer in a pool setting, the emotional side of the relationship may get shortchanged. The athlete will increasingly see the coach-athlete interaction as businesslike. The coach will tend to treat the athletes as objects for manipulation and direction. The coach will minimize, if not overlook completely, conversing with the athlete on matters that deal with life beyond the pool. Even in those situations in the pool when a different style of communication is required, and the coach attempts to make an emotional appeal (such as an exhortation to greater competitive effort), the appeal will fall on deaf ears. It will be viewed as "out of character." No groundwork will have been laid for the appeal to be effective. The coach will not recognize to which emotional cues one needs to be sensitive in order to appeal properly to the swimmer.

It is important to create settings in which various communicative styles can be used. The head coach can meet with the team for discussions on a variety of topics. In these sessions it is important to move away from a teaching mode. The coach should emphasize the likability style of communication. Coaches report that this style facilitates the development of team spirit, or cohesiveness, and allows individuals to learn about each other by focusing on experiences outside of swimming. These settings must be organized and clearly labeled as informal; a time to have fun. These sessions serve to counterbalance the emphasis on work which occurs in the pool. Studies of swimmers' (Gould et al. 1982) reasons for participating in the sport clearly indicate that having fun and developing social ties are among the more important items. As long as coaches incorporate social activities into the program structure which are fun and foster sociability, the attitude toward continued participation will be positive.

It is important to foster communication among team members. An effort should be made to encourage communication between newcomers (freshmen/transfers) and old-timers. If a strong tradition of upper-class leadership exists and newcomers are not expected to speak unless spoken to during training, the head coach must structure times when everyone can communicate freely. Another barrier that sometimes gets erected and stifles free flowing communication is the distinction between scholarship and non-scholarship athletes. If performances match with expectations, scholarship athletes can be turned to for leadership; if performances fall short of expectations, this type of status distinction can be a source of potential conflict. The coaching staff needs to try to minimize any discussion of scholarship as a basis for making invidious distinctions of worth.

Another strategy is to hold dialogues between the head coach and the swimmer. Such sessions build on ties started during recruitment and broaden the base of shared information. Both coach and swimmer develop a clearer understanding of the other's personal goals, the swimmer recognizes the rationale for the structure of the program, and the coach develops more complete information on the swimmer's goals and needs.

Research suggests that communication between individuals which fosters self-disclosure--revealing information of a personal nature--builds good relationships, enhances people's accuracy of perceptions of one another, and clarifies their understandings of one another's goals (Officer and Rosenfeld 1985: 360-70). Individuals who reveal personal information to others increase the risk that the other party may use that information against them. For disclosure to occur, the individual should see the listener as trustworthy, sincere, warm, and incapable of being provoked into using private information against anyone in a fit of anger. Individuals in positions of authority are less likely to be chosen as listeners than are individuals without authority. If the authority figure possesses these personality traits, then an individual might feel "free to open up." Parents are often selected as listeners; mothers are selected more often than fathers. Females are more frequently selected by females as listeners than are males, unless the male holds a job that is seen as providing technical knowledge, skills, or the ability to handle other people's problems--doctor, therapist, pharmacist (Hastings and Provol 1972), social worker, lawyer, teacher, or coach.

Coaches should recognize that females tend to engage in disclosure behavior more readily than do males. Females generally reveal matters concerning personal development and dealing with role identity to female coaches more easily than to males. Females will self-disclose to male coaches, if a foundation of trust has been established. The head coach, male or female, must recognize that the role of counselor automatically sets up an additional power dimension to that already claimed by virtue of the coach being an authority figure (Thorton 1981). By revealing personal information, the swimmer increases the degree of dependency on the coach. It is important that the coach not use this power in an exploitative fashion, if credibility as well as open and free-flowing communication are to be maintained.

It is important to recognize that simply providing different settings in which various types of communication might be manifested is no guarantee that, in fact, such styles of communication will occur. Athletes are shrewd enough to recognize that coaches may be manipulative; thus athletes are cynical concerning the coach's actions and intentions. Coaches, to be effective, must be sincere in order to ensure open communication.

The non-verbal message.-The non-verbal part of the message includes all actions other than the spoken part. It encompasses such actions as gestures, body posture, appearance, conduct, and the use of manipulation of physical objects and space which are extensions of self. Every social group shares understandings of what certain body postures or movements mean. Similarly, people from a particular culture recognize and agree on acceptable styles of dress, make-up, or costumes to be worn in given social settings. When certain types of clothes are worn, people expect that one should behave in a particular manner. How a person appears makes a moral statement to others, and indicates how an individual expects others to behave. Conversely, it also signals others on what kind of conduct one can expect in return.

Individuals as message senders are concerned with two elements of the act. First is the expression which is intended by the speaker. Second is the impression made on the audience. An individual, when transmitting a message consciously and unconsciously, uses both verbal and non-verbal elements. For there to be agreement between the expression created and the impression desired, there must be consistency between the spoken and unspoken parts of the message. The content must be clear and unambiguous. The sender must be sincere and convincing in conveying a message in order to ensure that the meaning is properly transmitted and that no misunderstanding occurs. Speech, appearance, and conduct must be consistent. Inconsistency creates ambiguity. Confusion may result between what is intended to be sent and what is received (Goffman 1959).

The head coach must be able to communicate clearly without distortion in order to convince swimmers that what is being said is truthful and important. The head coach should be able to manipulate personal expressions using whatever verbal styles, changes in appearance, or conduct are necessary to impress the audience addressed. In short, the head coach must be sensitive to the characteristics of the audience, whether an individual, a team, or a larger group with which he or she must communicate.

Recognizing the audience.-Who are the key people with whom the head coach must interact? What is the setting in which the communication will transpire? What role is to be played when communicating with this particular audience? What are the characteristics of the audience? What style of communication is expected?

A glance at Figure 1 reveals the different kinds of social relationships that the head coach establishes while occupying the coaching position in a university setting. Each relationship demands a different kind of role performance and a different style of

Figure 1.-Key People and Organizations Comprising the Social
Worlds of the College Swimming Coach

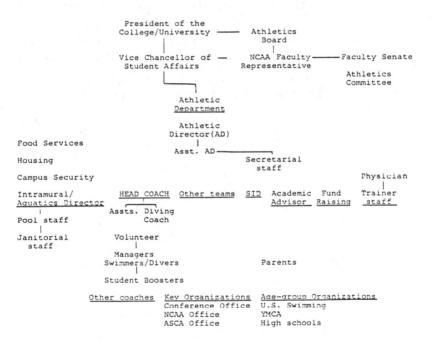

communicating. The types of activities expected in each of these roles are discussed in Chapters 7 and 8.[4]

Summary

--The head coach's role involves acting out two major role clusters: organizational and communication.

--The organizational role cluster encompasses a technical side involving such tasks as directing training and competition, running meets, recruiting swimmers, and selling the program inside and outside of the academic community. The organizational rule cluster also has a managerial side involving such tasks as administering personnel, planning the agenda for the entire program, handling the budget, and overseeing the clerical work.

--The communication role cluster deals with choosing the style of communication (problem-solving versus likability), manipulating settings in which interaction occurs, and determining the consistency and effectiveness of the message for the kind of audience addressed.

REVIEW QUESTIONS

1. What kinds of technical matters does a coach need to master in order to be competent?

2. What managerial tasks are the responsibility of the head coach?

3. Review Chapter 2 and determine what kinds of technical and managerial tasks can be delegated to assistant coaches and what tasks are better handled by the head coach.

4. What styles of communication do you think are most effective in working with swimmers? With staff? With people inside and outside of the sports community? Read Chapter 7 before answering the last question.

NOTES

[1]   Based on one's formal education, attendance at
clinics, professional reading and experience as an
apprentice, it is expected that coaches will become
familiar with and master information in the following
areas.

Understanding of principles of hydrodynamics and
applications in:
1. stroke mechanics for freestyle, backstroke,
butterfly, and breastroke
2. turn mechanics for each stroke and transitions for
individual medley
3. starts for individual races and relays
4. training for strokes; for sprinters, middle
distance, and distance
5. teaching techniques appropriate to individuals of
all ages from infants to Masters as well as use of
coaching aids and training aids

Principles of physiology and an understanding of
mechanics of body motion in:
6. recognition of symptoms of swimming injuries and
advantages and disadvantages of massage and rubdown
7. mechanics of dryland exercises
8. flexibility and mechanics of stretching
9. mechanics of isometric, isotonic, and isokinetic
training
10. conditioning and organization of phases of training
season--pre-season, competition, and tapering
11. principles of nutrition as well as consequences of
use of drugs

Understanding of selected principles in sociology and
psychology:
12. organization of competition schedule and meet
arrangements
13. models of control and decision making
14. models of organizational and interpersonal
communication
15. theories of learning and selected psychological
techniques--visualization, relaxation, motivation, goal
setting, bio-feedback
16. recognition of rhythm and sensory deprivation

Understanding business principles and work skills:
17. pool construction, maintenance, and management
18. microcomputer and data management software finances
19. finances, fund raising, and basic accounting.

This list of topics was compiled after reviewing topics covered in standard textbooks on teaching or coaching of competitive swimming, topics usually addressed in professional journals on swimming, and topics of major presentations or workshops at World Clinics conducted annually. Although the list is not exhaustive, it is representative.

2   Although I use some of Armistead categories, I do not adhere to his system rigidly.

3   An excellent discussion on the defining characteristics of behavioral modification in coaching is presented by Martin and Hrycaiko (1983).

4   The social relationship between the head coach and the NCAA faculty representative as well as the relationship of the head coach with and members of the various oversight committees are not discussed. First, not every institution has these positions. Second, among those schools that have such positions, the relationships are still undergoing negotiation and are not yet sufficiently defined as to permit discussion.

"Which scholarship did you finally accept, the one
to the University or the one to State?" (Karla)
"I decided to go to the University." (Carol)
"Why?" (Karla)
"Coach Mac is a great stroke technician. He is
personable. He is organized and has a good staff.
His practices are tough, but fun." (Carol)
"How come State turned you off?" (Karla)
"Coach T is a dictator. The program is almost
impossible. There is no room for personal
freedom. What ever Coach T says, you had better
do it or else you'll get pressure from everyone to
conform." (Carol)

"Hey, Curt. Have you ever met a coach who wasn't
self-assured, assertive, domineering, and thought
he could get along well with people?"
"You know, Heather. Every coach I've ever met
makes those claims. They generally see themselves
as more sociable than they really are."

* * * * * * * * * *

Just as observers note that the job of the head
coach has certain features that are fairly constant in
different settings from colleges to universities,
people sometimes ask whether there is a particular set
of personality traits which every coach possesses.
Simply put, people want to be able to distinguish
coaches from non-coaches.

Stereotypes and personality traits

Stereotypes.-Three different approaches are
typically noted in the effort to ascertain the
personality profiles of a coach. The first technique
is impressionistic reporting of personal observations
that stereotypes coaches in a particular sport.
Professionals with personal contact with coaches
generally stereotype the coach as "soulless," cool
under fire, "a meticulous dresser," team-oriented,
authoritarian (Scott 1969: 7), "insensitive,
...manipulative," and exploitative (Scott 1971: 134).
Similarly, Massengale (1974) marks coaches as
aggressive, highly organized, and unlikely to listen to
others. The mass media depicts coaches as muscular,
dominant, aggressive, sociable, and politically
conservative. Former players see some coaches as "to
the right of Attila the Hun." Ogilvie (1979: 47) adds

that coaches are ambitious, achievement-oriented, self-defined as leaders, assertive, hard-nosed, and risk-takers.

The second approach is psychological research to identify clusters of personality traits "unique" to a coach, a "successful" coach, or an "ideal" coach. A number of personality inventories have been developed, constructed, and administered by psychologists and sociologists to coaches in various sports, holding positions in youth sport programs, in junior and senior high schools, in colleges, and with national teams. The results of these studies roughly fall into two camps. One camp of researchers reports identifiable characteristics for coaches in particular sports (Hendry 1968; 1972). Another camp fails to find any set of personality traits that unambiguously differentiates coaches from non-coaches (see Sage 1980: 111-114; Sage 1975).

The third approach is research that: (1) compares athletes' perceptions of the "ideal" coach with the "actual" traits of the coach; (2) compares coaches' perceptions of traits of the ideal coach with self-reported traits (Hendry 1969); and (3) examines the congruency between coaches' and athletes' subjective and objective evaluations of each other (Hendry 1968). (These kinds of comparisons have also been used in studies of "preferred" or "ideal" styles of leadership.) Not surprisingly, swimmers agree on what traits make an "ideal coach." Similarly, coaches agree among themselves over what traits identify an "ideal coach." However, coaches' self-reports of personality traits tend toward self-aggrandizement. Athletes do not necessarily see the coach as possessing the same characteristics or as having the same amount of some characteristic as the coaches report. Coaches tend to give relatively lower evaluations of the character of athletes than do athletes themselves.[1]

Behavioral traits.-The coach-athlete relationship is the classic dyad of the leader and the led. Authority as leader is granted by the organization that hires or appoints the coach. The coach's duties are prescribed and proscribed by the organization. The coach is expected to supervise the program fulfilling the required organizational and communication roles. The taking care of these duties satisfies the coach's superiors.

For coaches to satisfy the athletes, they must be sensitive to the wants and needs of the athletes. If two people are in a goal-oriented situation, each must be willing to surrender something of their own wants and needs, either temporarily or for a longer period of time, in order to obtain a mutually desired outcome. In sports the desired ends are winning or continued improvement of current performances over past ones. Performance may be judged either objectively, such as times swum in an event, or subjectively, such as "I felt better today than I did yesterday."

Two approaches for looking at the coach-swimmer relationship are worth noting. The first approach sees the relationship as being influenced by situational factors, such as the nature of the task--its variability; the type of sport action--independence versus interdependence; the level and sources of stress--internal versus external; and the access to information flow--open versus limited.

The coaches' behaviors also are linked to the variability of the task. Low variability tasks are marked by closed action--skills performed in an environment where the stimuli are relatively stable, static, and unchanging. Training in an indoor pool is a closed action. The athlete's skills are routine and repetitious. The environment is relatively stable-- water temperature typically ranges from 78^0F to 82^0F, air temperature and light remain fixed. High variability tasks are characterized by open action-- where skills performed must adjust to shifts in the spatial/temporal environment of the athlete. Training or competing in the ocean is an open action. Wind, waves, and water temperature vary. Air temperature and sunlight change frequently. Currents, marine craft, and marine life are factors to which one must pay heed. Coaches who work in closed action sports tend to emphasize training behavior. A great deal of thought is required to vary the structure of workouts so that they are imaginative and interesting but still follow sound physiological principles of training. Coaches in open action sports spend a great deal of time preparing athletes to recognize situations and to be able to apply the proper strategy or play after reading the situational cues.

Coaches' behaviors in structuring a program differ depending on whether the sport emphasizes independence or interdependence of action by the athletes. Individual sports such as swimming and track foster the former; team sports such as basketball stress the later (Chelladurai and Saleh 1978). The nature of workouts reflects the demands of the sport. Swimmers can be given their workouts individually and only occasionally need to work together as members of a relay team. Some programs during examination week and finals will post workouts and allow swimmers to practice as their schedules permit. In fact, if an honor system is in effect at the school, the swimmers may be pledged to practice. Posting practices is feasible, although not preferable. Most swimmers complain that it is difficult to practice alone and sustain the same levels of mental concentration and physical effort in training as when one swims with someone else or with the team. To counteract this complaint, it is advisable to require that at least two swimmers train together. Basketball, football, hockey, and soccer, to note a few sports, demand that skill performances be practiced so that individuals adapt their actions to those of others (practice plays). In sum, the type of action and variability of the task influence the type of training behavior that a coach employs.

Two additional factors that influence the coach's behavior are the level of stress placed on athletes and coaches (Korten 1962) and the sources of stress-- internal versus external (Lott and Lott 1965). Under high-stress situations--such as preparing for an important dual meet with "the traditional rival," the conference championship, or a meet where swimmers are expected to qualify for national calibre championships- -the coach is likely to assume a greater degree of control. Conversely, under low-stress situations--such as a dual meet with a weaker team or a practice meet-- the coach is likely to become more easy-going. Both styles of maintaining control are effective in achieving the best performances for individuals and the team.

Similarly, the degree of control required may also depend on the level of stress produced by the point at which the team is during the season. In the beginning of the season, the athletes are adjusting to school and practices emphasize general conditioning; stress tends to be relatively low. The coach needs to maintain enough control to provide guidance so that athletes and staff can fit into the program and know their roles and goals. Once a routine is established the coach can ease the reins until the competitive phase of the season. Once competition begins, control needs to be tightened as new activities are mastered--such as training and competing without tapering,[2] learning the format of collegiate meets, learning to juggle travel and studies, and learning how to deal with the press. Once newcomers become veterans, the controls can be eased again. Finally, control needs to be exercised in preparation for the championship part of the season. This part of the season is the culmination of everyone's efforts. A coach's job security is tied to team performance. To surrender control and increase the likelihood of unwanted but preventable events affecting performance is not rational behavior for the coach.

Where the sources of stress are external, the coach must be able to focus the attention of individuals on group goals. This strategy is: "Don't worry what the papers are saying. The press tends to blow things out of proportion. All we need to do is to concentrate on the task at hand. Let's get it together and perform up to our capabilities." The coach acts as a facilitator.

Where the sources of stress are internal, the coach must evaluate the skill levels of individuals, must pay attention to individuals' wants, anxieties, and problems. The coach must also recognize the strengths and weaknesses of particular clique combinations in order to ameliorate problems and ensure a cohesive team effort. The abilities of listening and communicating, using both reason and emotion, are critical for the coach's survival and growth as a successful professional.

Another situational factor affecting the coach-swimmer relationship is the degree of access to information flow. When the coach and swimmer obtain sufficient information from each other or from the assistant coaches and outside parties, then decisions reached will tend to be more effective since whatever contingencies could be identified will have been considered. When people feel that they are fully informed, then their level of satisfaction generally is higher than when their access to information is restricted.

The second approach focuses on leadership behavior. Behavioral scientists are interested in ascertaining what behaviors are displayed by successful leaders that ensure worker satisfaction and effective group performance. Sociologists in industry, the military, and in various organizational settings as well as students of small group processes have long focused on what personality traits mark the successful leader. This same issue resurfaces in the investigation of leadership in sports. Research on personality characteristics of leaders generally fails to identify any clear-cut set of traits that predisposes an individual toward emerging into greatness as a coach.

Behavioral scientists have also asked a second and closely related question on leadership: If there are no intrinsic personality traits typifying successful leaders, then are there any behaviors that all successful leaders share across all settings? Further, are these behaviors universal or limited to a particular setting? Regardless of which of the two questions is posed, the intent of research has been to identify the kinds of behavior that would make the coach more effective in relating to the team, increasing the satisfaction of athletes, and enhancing team performance. Inventories of behaviors have been constructed and respondents asked for their perceptions of leadership behaviors found in a "good" coach, "all" coaches, or that are "preferred" in coaches. Various studies (Halpin and Winer 1957; Fleishman 1957a, 1957b; Danielson et al. 1975; Hendry 1972; Chelladurai and Saleh 1978) suggest that good training behavior and the ability to exercise control are behaviors that coaches are expected to possess. Training behavior is "aimed at improving the performance level of athletes by emphasizing and facilitating hard and strenuous training, clarifying the relationships among members" (Carron 1980). The style of training behavior used by the coach is linked to the swimmers' events. Distance swimmers who require more mileage tend to have long, boring, and often repetitive sets. Sprinters have shorter, more varied, and interesting workouts. Personal observation and research show that swimmers' perceptions of the coach's training behavior are important. Swimmers expect that coaches will emphasize training as part of their leadership responsibilities. When swimmers become fatigued they may complain, but failure of coaches to stress training is taken as a sign of weakness.

Styles of leadership

The exercise of control deals with decision making (Chelladurai and Haggerty 1978). Coaches might operate in one of four modes of decision making: autocratic--the coach makes all the decisions; consultative--the coach shares problems with athletes and the subordinates asking for their input, then makes the decision; participative--the coach talks with subordinates collectively and everyone votes; or delegative--the coach assigns the decision to a subordinate and the coach merely serves to implement

78

the decision of the subordinate. Vroom and Yetton (1973) suggest that four conditions affect the selection of a decision making mode: (1) quality requirement--the coach's expertise needed in reaching a judgment; (2) information--access to all the facts needed in making a decision; (3) complexity of the problem--judgment needed on one best option among many that assesses the relative merits and demerits of strategies, strengths, and weaknesses of personnel; and (4) group integration--judgment needed on how to reduce conflict on a team. Chelladurai and Arnott (1985) found that: (1) a delegative style was rejected by most athletes; (2) females prefer a participative style more so than do males; (3) athletes are willing to yield to the coach on complex issues or when the coaches have information and athletes do not; and (4) athletes also would rather defer to the authority of the coach than to their fellow athletes.

Regardless of what research suggests, one of the more difficult issues to resolve as a beginning coach is how much control to assert in structuring the program as well as on the lives of the athletes and the coaching staff. Also, the coach must decide how control should be effected over those key individuals with whom one must interact inside and outside of the university.

Usually the choice of decision-making style is a result of the personality characteristics of the coach as well as the influences of the various institutional pressures. A coach opting for the autocratic mode becomes the team general. In this style the coach sets the goals for the program and decides where the program will rank in the conference at the end of the year and in five years. Where national ranking is expected, the coach sets the agenda and means for achieving that end. The coach schedules the dual meets for the season, deciding whether the schedule will be easy or hard. If the conference is tough, some coaches include weaker schools from outside of the conference in order to compile an acceptable win and loss record. If an autocratic coach wants to build a reputation for the program as one that competes against only the elite, then the coach will only schedule meets with nationally ranked teams.

The autocratic coach oversees the role of the assistant coaches, dictating responsibilities and parameters within which decisions are permissible. The role of manager is structured as a recorder of splits, equipment caretaker, and ubiquitous "go-getter."

This coach maintains rigid control over the athletes' lives both in the pool and outside. The coach dictates practice hours and discourages swimmers from taking courses with labs or field work that conflict with pool time. Standards are set for a team dress code while on or off campus. The code may apply only during the season or for the entire academic year. The coach may discourage or perhaps prohibit any conversation with outsiders on matters related to swimming such as--the nature of workouts; meet performances; actions of swimmers, coaches, and staff; or any decisions related to the program.

The autocratic coach moves to establish control over anybody and anything that might impinge on the program. In handling the press, all interviews are filtered through the coach's office. In dealing with the physician and training staff, the coach double checks all diagnoses and therapies to see if malingering has occurred or if therapies can be intensified in order to speed recovery. In working with the AD, social distance is maintained wherever possible. Autonomy is absolutely mandatory.

Academic advisors are carefully screened by the autocratic coach. If advisors are helpful, the coach will work with them. If not, the coach will take over the advisor's duties and make sure that the needs of the swimmers and divers are fulfilled. Whenever possible the coach will hire a personal secretarial staff and will make sure preferred janitors get assigned to the pool venue. All information that pertains to the team must be channeled through the coach's office. When individuals do not support the program, the coach figures out ways to eliminate them or to get around them. Alternative personnel are used or the coach informally usurps the responsibilities of others so that control of the program remains firmly grasped.

A real problem is that domination of all parties is enervating and runs a high risk of loss of personal control, especially if other parties refuse to cooperate. Such a tactic breeds a mentality of crisis management since each problem must be handled by the coach alone. People must be contacted, manipulated, and aligned so that the desired outcome is guaranteed.

Given the number of duties of the head coach, both role strain and role overload are real possibilities for the autocratic coach. Multiple workouts each day, meetings, recruiting, administrative chores, and so forth can easily reduce even the most physically fit and driven coach to a state of exhaustion unless some of the responsibilities are delegated (Daland 1975: 48).

A coach who opts for a consultative or participative mode reduces the level of stress that is self-imposed. The head coach reaches decisions on the overall structure of the program, scheduling, and so forth, and then allocates assignments to the coaching staff and support personnel. Allocations usually follow open and free exchanges with the individuals involved. The program goals and philosophy are explained to the team; individual goals are negotiated. Control rests with the head coach, but there is a recognition by the coach that a good leader also is led. In following this strategy, the head coach recognizes that people who work with the program can best be handled by adhering to an equity principle in social exchanges. "You give me something, and I will reciprocate." This style reduces tension among individuals that have to interact with the coach. Also, burnout in the coaching staff, athletes, and support personnel is less likely to occur under the consultative and participative modes than under the autocratic mode.

To be effective coaches must establish a working relationship with athletes. If no relationship exists, the issue of whether a coach operates from an autocratic, consultative, or participative mode is irrelevant. Further, whether the coach displays warmth and supportive behavior toward the athletes is also moot. For control to be effective and any affection displayed, and seen as sincere, a relationship must persist. Usually, compatibility is more easily achieved the longer a swimmer remains with the program. Swimmers who are incompatible leave the program voluntarily, become targets of derision and harassment to force conformity, or simply are cut from the team (Carron and Bennett 1977).

The decision over which mode to choose also must be tempered by a cognizance of the personalities of the athletes. If the athletes seek a dependency relationship with a coach, then the autocratic mode may work best. Conversely, athletes who eschew authority tend to prefer a participative mode. Coaches should recognize the mode of decision making that they employ and try to recruit to develop a match in personality styles between staff and athletes.

81

Organizational substitutability and problems of turnover

One problem in any organization and over which a coach must establish control is the phenomenon of personnel turnover. Some programs are marked by <u>high</u> turnover. For instance, programs that depend on volunteer and part-time paid assistant coaches generally have a complete turnover of personnel every two or three years. In a program with high turnover, the head coach spends a great deal of time instructing assistants. Thus, swimmers are required to adjust to new personnel. Each time there is a shift in staff, there is the potential for new coalitions, friendships, and conflicts to form. New assistants constantly have to adjust to a program with which the swimmers already are familiar. When an assistant makes an error, the seasoned swimmer can correct or sometimes even belittle the assistant with impunity, undermining the credibility of the assistant. This strategy is more likely to be employed where swimmers do not respect or like the assistant. In cases where all the assistants happen to be new in a given year, swimmers can play on inexperience creating a variety of possible problems among the staff.

Older assistants can use their seniority and familiarity with the program to establish a pecking order among the assistant coaches. Old-timers can withhold information in order to sabotage the performance of new assistants. Conversely, old-timers can serve as sources of information for newcomers, relieving some of the pressure on the head coach.

The problem of turnover in a program is exacerbated when the assistant diving coach is temporary (a graduate assistant). For instance, the assistant diving coach is expected to recruit divers. For the temporary assistant diving coach this may be difficult since diving recruits will enter the program at the same time a new assistant does. New divers will be subject to a new and different assistant. The astute diving recruits recognize that they might end up working with three, and possibly four, assistant diving coaches during four years of eligibility (1--the assistant doing the recruiting, 2--the assistant who arrives in the program as the diver enters as a freshmen, 3--the assistant who enters the program while the diver is a junior, and possibly 4--if one the assistants quits school for some reason).

Frequent turnover of diving assistants also makes it difficult for the diver to adjust to different sets of coaching cues used when learning new dives or correcting diving mechanics. The change in diving coaches also requires readjustment between coaches and divers as new interactive styles are encountered.

Turnover also occurs among athletes. Each year there is attrition as swimmers find that they have underestimated the magnitude of work and pressure in a program. Some find that the role conflict between student and athlete needs to be resolved in favor of academics. Others develop conflicts with the coaching staff, with other athletes, or with individuals outside of the team, such as boyfriends or girlfriends. They may suffer injuries or become ill. By the time an incoming class reaches its senior year, very few of the original group remain.

The head coach needs to reiterate each year the basic principles of the program, its major goals, the duties of the staff and the responsibilities of the swimmers in order to ensure continuity. Without repetition newcomers find it difficult to discern the structure of the program. In such cases role assignments only get developed through trial and error. To avoid ambiguity and misunderstandings by the staff and swimmers over role expectations, the head coach needs to delineate the job tasks of each and must inform the staff and swimmers of their assigned responsibilities.

Some programs have <u>low</u> turnover. For instance, the head assistant coach and other assistants stay with the program for a number of years. Graduate assistants remain with the program through both the Master's and Ph.D. degree programs. Some even remain with the university and volunteer their services after graduation.

To ensure stability and continuity in a program, there must be a paid full-time assistant coach. Continuity in a position increases familiarity with the program and fosters a better understanding of role responsibilities of the head and assistant coaches. Clarity of roles allows staff, swimmers, and administration to identify who is responsible for which duties and who is to be held accountable for which acts of omission and commission.

Philosophy of management

Even a cursory review of the literature on coaching suggests two different foci in setting the tone of the program.

First is the <u>product-oriented</u> program. The expressed goal is to produce as many nationally-ranked and world-class swimmers as humanly possible. The coaching staff sets up an age-graded program that is integrated so that swimmers progress through stages from simple techniques to more refined techniques, from low yardage to high yardage, and from less competitive to more competitive meets. Efforts are made to incorporate as many swimmers as feasible in each rung of the program in order to ensure that quality "bubbles to the top." The coaching staff is not overly concerned with attrition. The program will survive, as most institutions do. After all, the long-recognized principle of organizations operates: the larger the organization, the more substitutable individuals become. This approach emphasizes mass production as the means and ranked performances as the product.

Second is the <u>person-oriented</u> program. The expressed goal is to create swimmers who are fundamentally sound in mechanics and who swim to achieve their potential. The same age gradations and stages exist, but the individual rather than the group becomes the unit of attention. Attrition is an indicator of a misalignment between the individual's priorities and those of the program; a compromise is needed for solution. In this program the individual is not substitutable. This approach emphasizes "crafting" as the means and "self-actualization" as the end (ASCA 1986: 15-21).

These two approaches as presented describe extremes on a continuum. In actual practice most programs, depending on the numbers of swimmers, the availability of assistant coaches, physical resources, and most especially time, are a mixture of these characteristics that fall somewhere between the two extremes. Although I have no data to support this supposition, I believe that coaches who emphasize technique, try to expand the swimmer's awareness of self and others, and see coaching as an art form appear to favor the "people end" of the continuum. In contrast, coaches who emphasize technique, espouse excellence through subjugation of pain and mastery over adversity, and see coaching as a practical application of scientific principles appear to favor the "product approach."

Whatever blend of management styles is effected the coach should remain humble. Scientific research continually expands the horizons of knowledge, out-dating prior truths. New principles and applications devolve from these findings. Experimentation yields new techniques which later are incorporated under the umbrella of some new scientific paradigm[3] and the reason for their working is explained. The same attrition of ideas and blossoming of fads that occurs among the scientists also takes place among the coaches.

Coaches tend to become enamored with new thoughts and new practices just like everyone else. Sometimes boredom, the desire to experiment, or sheer forgetfulness will lead a coach to discard something old which worked, for something new that may not be as successful. Occasionally, coaches recognize that an error has been made and the old ways are revived.

No matter how happy the coach is with the structure of the program or the efficacy of techniques used, the nature of the effect of a coach on a swimmer has not been unequivocally fixed. Clearly, new skills are transmitted and improvements in swimmers' technique are demonstrable. But less certain are changes in swimmers' motivations or in their abilities to cope with anxieties and engage in problem-solving behavior. The coach can act as an information source, exposing the swimmer to new ways of addressing self and the environment. The coach also can act as a facilitator, assisting the swimming in utilizing these methodologies. The athlete has to be receptive to learning and trying these methodologies for them to be able to be useful.

It is safe to assume that athletes who want to change are probably more open to direction and suggestion than those who are rigid. The effect of the program on values or behavioral changes of any permanence in building character is open to question. So also is the actual role of the coach as an effective counselor. There are not any systematic studies that evaluate long-term changes in behavior due to participation in intercollegiate competitive swimming versus non-participation. Until research identifies what kinds of changes occur and their relative magnitudes, the coach will increase the likelihood of success by establishing a compatible relationship with the swimmer. Change in the direction desired is more likely to occur where compatibility exists than where the coach and swimmer do not get along.

One of the best ways to ensure compatibility is to pay especial attention to recruiting.

Summary

--Coaches generally are stereotyped by former athletes and by the media as muscular, dominant, aggressive, risk-takers, and control-oriented personalities. Research to identify personality traits questions the accuracy of popularly held stereotypes.

--Research on coach-athlete interaction suggests that coaches' behavior is influenced by situational factors--such as the nature of task variability, type of sport action, sources and levels of stress, and access to information flow.

--Research on leadership behaviors of coaches, a tradition borrowed from studies of organizations, shows that athletes want coaches (1) to stress training behavior to enhance performance and (2) to exercise control over the program.

--Studies of decision-making styles suggest that autocratic and consultative modes are preferred by coaches and athletes over participative and delegative modes. The type of control effected by coaches depends on their philosophy of management, whether it is product- or person-oriented.

--One issues that inevitably is faced by college and university coaches is the turnover of personnel. To reduce the problem, program goals and structure as well as roles of swimmers and staff must be clearly articulated by the head coach.

REVIEW QUESTIONS

1. Check the literature on attitude and behavior traits that a swim coach actually, ideally, or preferably should possess. Chelladurai's Leadership Scale is one possible choice. Answer the questions in two ways: (1) What attitudes or behaviors do you like in a coach; and (2) Do you possess these attitudes and behaviors?

2. What range of factors influence a coach's leadership style?

3. What kind of leadership style would you use as a coach? What kind of style would you prefer as an athlete?

4. What factors influence personal turnover among the staff and among the swimmers? What steps should a coach take to reduce problems associated with high turnover?

5. What kind of management philosophy do you favor-- product-oriented or people-oriented? Defend your choice.

NOTES

[1] Much of the effort to identify the personality profile of coaches by behavioral scientists is a reflection of tensions seen in society at large. In part, the effort was an extension of behavioral scientists to identify personality makeup of people in any leadership position. After World War II there was an attempt to distinguish between people with a predisposition toward either an authoritarian or democratic personality. Some critics viewed this effort as a witch hunt to root out and prevent another debacle like that which occurred in Germany. In part, the effort is a reaction to the social rebellion against institutional forms of control that marked the 1960s and 1970s. Coaches who operated in an autocratic fashion were targeted as being out of step with more liberal tendencies of student representation and self-direction. Students and athletes allegedly wanted to demythologize those values that gave rise to the Vietnam involvement and wanted to effect some degree of control over their lives through direct participation in various institutions. Coaches who operated autocratically were pressured to change to consultative or participative styles of leadership.

[2] Learning to swim fast while involved in heavy training is not the usual experience of swimmers recruited from U.S. Swimming and YMCA age-group experience. Swimmers who compete for prep schools or high schools or simultaneously train with age-group programs and swim for prep/high schools may be exposed to this kind of meet schedule. In general, freshmen must learn to adjust to the dual meet season.

[3] For the reader interested in the philosophy of science and sensitive to the notion of paradigms, a comparison of the different vocabularies, ways of thinking, and explanations of swimming mechanics, see Seals and Hastings (Forthcoming).

"Hey, Marcelle. Are you going to visit the University of T?"
"Why should I? The program is not even ranked."

"I never heard a thing from any university or college swimming program until I placed at NJOs. Now, I regularly get newsletters from about 20 programs."

"When I was little I went to swim camp at the University. Ever since then, I have dreamed about swimming for Coach T."

"Jane, how did your visit go this weekend?"
"It was really great. The coach is open and really concerned. The kids are easy to get to know. I got to meet a lot of people. The party Saturday night was awesome."

"Will you go if they make you an offer?'
"I'm going even if I have to walk-on."

****

The organizational role of the coach includes both a technical dimension and a managerial dimension. By far, the technical side involves the most time and energy to learn, to stay current with new ideas and practices, and to conduct the day-to-day round of activities. One of the more time consuming aspects of the technical side of coaching is recruiting. A lot of ink has been spilled over the sins committed by coaches when attempting to convince athletes to attend their particular institution and swim for them, but relatively few descriptions exist that identify what coaches do at each step of the process.

The recruiting process

Steps involved.-Recruiting is one of the most important role responsibilities of a coach. Recruits are the lifeblood of a program. At the very least, they are needed to maintain a program and to replace swimmers lost for various reasons.[1] At best, recruits are the vehicle for improving the quality of the program. Typically, successful recruiting in many programs improves the coach's job security. To move into the top echelon of competition the coach has to be able to convince "blue chippers" to attend the

institution.   Given the current state of
intercollegiate athletics where many schools compete
for the services of an individual athlete, programs
that already have an elite reputation have the edge in
the bidding process.   The rich get richer and get the
"blue chipper."   The others get the "pale blue
chipper."

1. Who is out there?-The head coach and an
assistant coach usually are responsible for recruiting.
Recruiting first and foremost is an exercise in
information gathering.   There are two types of
information sources: organizational sources which
include lists published by various swimming
associations and lists produced by private enterprise;
and informal networks which include information
available to the coach through alumni, friends, and
supporters of the program.   Organizational sources are
relatively easy to identify.   Each year various lists
of swimmers are produced.   These lists include: (1)
High School All Americans; (2) Prep School All
Americans; (3) YMCA National Meet Times; (4) National
Junior Olympics Meet Times; (4) Top Times among Age-
Groupers: and (5) Top Times in the World.   These lists
usually can be obtained from Swimming World and Junior
Swimmer in the July and August issues.   Also available
from other countries are international and national
meet results and top performances.   For instance, Swim
Canada lists top performances among age-groupers for
the various provinces.   Also available are lists of
various high schools and prep schools and their
coaches, U.S. Swimming clubs and the coaches, and some
YMCA programs and the coaches.

Informal sources take time to cultivate.   The
coach must spend time and energy creating support for
the program.   Ties with various booster organizations,
alumni, and fans must be developed.   Ties with former
swimmers need to be sustained.   Once a support network
is in place, these various people often send names,
news clippings, and make calls in order to tell the
coach of an up and coming prospect for the program.   In
some cases swimmers or divers who were recruited
elsewhere, signed, tried the program and withdrew are
identified by alumni, former swimmers, or friends of
the university.   This information often is an important
addition to that obtained from organizational sources.

2. Preparation of a master file.- With the
use of these lists and by calling coaches with whom
swimmers train, the head coach and the assistant coach
can produce a master file that contains the swimmer's

name, age, class in school, home address, home phone, events and performances, swim club, coach, club/school address, club phone, student's GPA, SAT, or ACT scores, and other data as desired. In the past coaches recorded this information in file folders or on an index card. Today this information is more easily stored on a computer file or disk file and manipulated using a standard data base management system. There is a variety of good data management systems available for personal computers. If the head coach is not familiar with computers and programming, but one the assistants is, then the head coach should delegate to that assistant the responsibilities for entering data and updating the records. If no one on the staff is prepared to handle computers, find a student in the computer sciences department or a work study student with these skills. The time saved in using the computer is worth the cost. It is best to prepare the master recruit file so that it can be sorted on any desired characteristic. For instance, if the head coach is looking for a breaststroker, the master file can be keyed to list all persons who swim the breast stroke.

3. Screening.-Once the file has been generated, it is sorted by class in school and sex to ascertain which recruits are seniors and eligible. Those individuals who are juniors or younger are tracked. Their performances in meets are recorded along with any honors achieved. Letters congratulating them for their achievements are regularly sent to let them know that the program is interested in them. To accomplish this mailing, standard form letters can be created. With the use of a merge and sort routine, names, addresses, and personal information can be integrated into the standard letter. A variety of software packages are available for personal computers that can handle these tasks. As further advances are made in personal computers and in the field of desk-top publishing, this part of the recruiting process will become more sophisticated, flexible, and faster.

Senior swimmers' files--high school and prep school--are examined for event and performance, test scores, and GPA in order to ascertain whether they are scholastically eligible under the minimum standards specified by NCAA Proposition #48, and whether their performances are competitive enough for the program. If swimmers pass this initial screening, a letter and questionnaire are sent to them along with general information on the university. The questionnaire solicits information that helpful in assessing the students' level of preparation academically and athletically. Special interests also are probed, so that any follow-up communications can make use of the information in order to establish rapport between the coach and the athlete. Swimmers interested in the program fill out the questionnaire and return it.

Once any contact has been made between the athlete and any agent of the university, a file should be started and kept on that individual. Contacts by phone, letter, or personal visits should be documented with a brief description of who represented the school, what transpired, and the date. This procedure of maintaining files is helpful in aiding the coaching staff to adhere to NCAA guidelines when recruiting. Such materials also are useful as evidence should NCAA inquiries be made into program practices.

4. Getting the athlete in the pipeline.-A letter of acknowledgment is sent thanking the student for interest in the program. A college or university catalogue is sent with an admissions package, which includes an application form and information on academic scholarships. If the admissions office and the athletic department cooperate in the process of recruiting, the coach will contact the admissions office to request that this package be sent to the athlete. The swimmer is invited to apply for admission to the institution. When the application is received, the admissions office informs the coach. An admissions officer sends a NCAA form to the high school to have the student's list of core courses, GPA in those courses, and overall GPA verified. The admissions officer checks grades, and SAT or ACT scores to determine if the minimum academic performance requirements are satisfied.

5. Keeping contact.-If the swimmer is interested or has applied, then contact is made on a regular basis throughout the senior year by mail and phone. Mail-outs to recruits tend to stress information about the athletic program, the swim team's progress and performance, and personal news on particular swimmers. Any available newsletters are routinely sent.

Newsletters are sent to recruits, adult and student boosters, alumni of the swimming programs--age-groupers, clinic attenders, and former team members, officials, and individuals who have expressed even a vague interest in the program. (Parents of swimmers receive the newsletter regularly along with others on

92

the list.) Newsletters contain items on the dual meet schedule (home and away) as well as sites and dates of conference championships and nationals. Where special arrangements can be made for food and lodging at reduced rates for athletic functions, the newsletter indicates which hotels and motels are cooperating with the athletic department or the school and the name of the person to contact for reservations. Plans for special events—such as the team banquet, orientation party, or parents' weekend—also are included.

At the beginning of the year new additions to the squad are introduced and their expected contributions to the team's performance noted. This publicity release provides an opportunity for the coach to set some public goals for the athletes. (Sometimes the goals are a surprise to the athletes beyond their earlier estimations of their abilities. The fact that goals are openly stated gives the athletes something to which to aspire.) During the year progress with training, set-backs due to injuries and general interest stories are released. During the competition phase of the season, the team record is noted and regularly updated. Outstanding performances are highlighted. Weaknesses in the team are obvious by their omission. An astute recruit will recognize those events in which a team needs help. When team news is slow the newsletter can be used to educate the audience on the team's philosophy, to explain some of the technical parts of the program, or to introduce the coaching staff.

The head coach can delegate the preparation of the newsletter to an assistant coach who writes well. Since the newsletter represents the team and an academic institution, it is imperative to edit it. Typos, syntax errors, poor diction, and slang are to be avoided. Recruits who receive a newsletter filled with errors or quotations from the coach that smack of illiteracy may decide to look at another program. If coaches cannot write, the head coach should find an English or communication major to do the job. Better yet, if the sports information office is large enough, turn the task of preparing newsletters over to them.

Phone calls emphasize personal interest in the swimmer, keeping abreast of the swimmer's progress, and developing a feel for the swimmer's personality. Phone contacts vary in number for each recruit. Some like to be called frequently and it is necessary for the coach to maintain a high level of contact in order to demonstrate that the program remains interested.

Others would rather be left alone and will reach their decision without continued pressure. Many coaches use phone contacts as an opportunity to develop rapport with other members of the family. In some cases coaches find it more profitable to talk with the parents instead of the athletes. Others feel the opposite is true.

Phone contacts are a rewarding part of the process, but they are time consuming and often require long hours at night or on the weekends. Many high school seniors are difficult to reach either early in the evening or during the week. There also may be differences between time zones to which one must accommodate.

6. The visit.-If a swimmer is interested in visiting a campus, arrangements are made for a visit. Recruits may be assigned to a host/hostess--swimmer or diver. In some cases a coach or another agent of the university may escort the recruit while on campus. Visits tend to be exercises in "stage management" by creating a schedule of events, circumstances, and personalities that display the university and the program in the best possible light.

In orchestrating the visit the coach must take into account the student-athlete's interests: possible major, hobbies, and friends who attend the school. Meetings with academic representatives, with appropriate administrators, and with friends are scheduled. (Incidentally, it is important to build a pool of faculty and administrators who will help with recruiting. Make sure that they are protagonists of sport and sympathetic to the swimming program. See the section in Chapter 8 on coping with the faculty.) The itinerary is structured so that the recruit gets a chance to ask questions about the university and the athletic program, to see the physical layout of the school, and to develop a feeling for the rhythm of daily life by watching practices and attending classes. The recruit also has an opportunity to sample the social life.

When the swimmer visits campus, whether early in the fall or immediately before signing date in the spring, is a matter that needs to be judged by the coach based on a reading of the recruit's interest in the school versus other programs. It is not clear whether first impressions or last impressions are most important in shaping the decision to attend a school or not. Most recruits usually visit during the fall,

94

winter, and spring, but rarely during the summer. Statistics indicate that for those athletes that eventually attend a particular school, roughly two-thirds had visited on a recruiting trip. Thus, a visit is important for the recruit's decision to attend a school.

Some coaches feel that it is more important for the recruits to get to know the coaching staff on the visit, since these are the individuals who will be structuring their lives during the next four years of eligibility. Conversely, some coaches feel that it is more important for the recruit to develop rapport with the swimmers. In many cases, these will be the people with whom one rooms, eats, trains, studies, and parties. Regardless of the emphasis used in organizing the visit, it is important that the recruit always have something scheduled and an escort acting as guide and host.

Visits may be scheduled to coincide with a special event--such as a football game between major rivals, Homecoming, parents' weekend, or a party weekend. If two schools are wooing the same recruit, a coach may invite the recruit for a visit when these schools compete. This strategy has a high risk, and usually finds that the winner takes all.

Recruiting focuses on establishing rapport between the coach, the athlete and the family. Often it is important to solicit support of one or both parents, convincing them that the school and the program are ideally suited to the academic and athletic needs of their son or daughter.

7. Getting a verbal commitment.-After the mail-outs, phone calls, and visits, the head coach and assistants attempt to assess the chances that the swimmer will decide to attend the school and swim for the program and that the parents will agree with the athlete's decision. Based on the athlete's interest in the program, the rapport with the coaches and the swimmers, the evaluation of the program, and the merits of the academic opportunities and social life, an inclination is solicited from the athlete on whether he/she is leaning toward or away from coming. Those not favorably inclined are asked which programs they like best in order to assess whether their commitment is firm or whether they should still be courted. Where rejection is firm, the connection cools.

Those athletes favorably inclined or ambivalent are further courted and attempts are made to overcome any doubts concerning the school or program. Even if an athlete verbally commits to the program, the coaching staff recognizes that nothing is assured until the athlete signs a letter of intent (if a scholarship is offered) or enrolls for courses, attends, and shows up for practice when the training season begins. Even then some swimmers drop out of the program.

8. Signing.-In programs where athletic scholarships are offered to student-athletes, the goal of the entire process of recruitment is signing. Some coaches tender a scholarship offer by mailing contracts to the athletes, then await responses as of a specified deadline. Other coaches contact those individuals who have made a verbal commitment and set up a visit in the recruits' homes so that the athletes can sign letters of intent indicating they will attend the school and accept the scholarship offered.

Once athletes have signed, they cannot compete for other schools without a release from the institution with which they signed. Coaches differ over who represents the program and the school when signing the athlete. In some cases assistant coaches take this responsibility, in others it is strictly the domain of the head coach. Often it depends on which coach has worked the longest with the recruit during the process of recruiting. When dealing with the "blue chipper" most head coaches, funds permitting, make the trip to sign. Roundy and Roh (1973) find that approximately two-thirds of top basketballers have been visited either by the head coach or the freshman coach. Based on limited conversations with swim coaches, most feel that home visits are critical in the recruiting process. Over the years a higher proportion of athletes who have been visited at home end up attending the school than athletes simply contacted by mail and phone. The personal touch is mandatory.

The funnel effect versus the wedding cake.-The number of athletes who are screened, contacted by mail, fill out questionnaires, fill out admission applications, visit, get accepted, and are tendered a scholarship, accept, and show up on campus varies. The process of recruiting acts like a "funnel." Initially several hundreds of athletes may be screened. A few hundred may be contacted by mail and asked to fill out questionnaires. A large portion screen themselves out of further contacts by refusing to return a questionnaire. From the remaining pool of returns, some refuse to send in an application for admission. Of the applicants, a few or many (depending on admission standards at the school) may not get accepted. From the recruits admitted, a small sub-set represents potential scholarship material. Among those who are tendered a contract, some may decline and go elsewhere. Some sign and may not show up on campus. If the arrive on campus a few may decline to swim and drop out of the program.

No study swimmers exists which systematically examines the proportionate losses at each stage from the original pool of athletes screened, controlling for division, academic reputation, rank of the program, gender, and reputation of the athletic program across all sports. From conversations with coaches at meets and conventions, it appears that the magnitude of losses from the initial screening to acceptance and actual participation are greatest in institutions with outstanding academic reputations and/or those that do not offer scholarships.

Another way of thinking of the pool of recruits, besides the funnel effect, is the image of a wedding cake.[2] The wedding cake is constructed of three layers. The top layer is small. It contains the elite swimmers, the "blue chippers." These swimmers have been competitive internationally and nationally as age-groupers and interscholastic swimmers. As freshmen they will score in the NCAA championships. They will bring instant visibility to the program. These are the individuals who receive the full brunt of the school's attention as well as attention from all the major swimming programs in the country. The head coach takes full responsibility for contacting them, making phone calls, and visiting their homes. Wherever they sign, they will receive full rides.

The middle layer is larger. It contains well-seasoned swimmers, the "pale blue chippers." These individuals will make a solid contribution to the program, probably winning in dual meet competition, and scoring in conference championships. As freshmen they may qualify for NCAAs as a member of one of the relay teams. By the time they become upperclassmen they should qualify in individual events. Depending on the competitiveness of the program, they may receive full rides or partial scholarships.

The bottom layer of the cake is the biggest. It contains experienced swimmers. They are good competitors, but have yet to make a showing in major competition. These are the swimmers with potential who may mature once involved in a rigorous program. They may place or show in dual competition or score a few points in consolations in conference meets. They may earn partial scholarships.

There is nothing pejorative about this ranking system. Judgments are made based on available information. Sometimes "blue chippers" wash out. Conversely, sometimes walk-ons develop into top flight athletes. Athletes at each level contribute to the overall strength of the program. The more swimmers with which a coach has to work, the stronger the team will be in both dual and championship competition. The more depth a team has, the greater the flexibility in training and assigning individuals to events. With the new scoring system which emphasizes depth, coaches will have to fill their plates with pieces of cake from each tier.

Strategies of recruiting

"Selling the athlete."-How coaches choose to recruit is a matter of personal style and preference. Some coaches believe that "you tell the athlete whatever he or she wants to hear." The point of the exercise is to get the athlete on campus. Most recruits are not going to be sophisticated enough to disentangle fact from fiction, will be awed by the process, and will not ask the right kinds of questions concerning academic requirements, availability of programs, excellence of majors, eating and housing plans, insurance and medical coverage, and so forth until they get home. The visit often appears as a blur to the recruits. So many activities are packed into a brief period of time that there is no opportunity to assimilate all the information being presented. Following a visit, recruits when telling their parents about the school will often recognize that many of the questions that were supposed to have been asked, were not. Recruit then call in order to fill in the missing pieces.

Such an approach assumes that once athletes begin school as a freshmen they can form their own opinions based on personal experiences. If a freshmen is disgruntled and cannot adjust to the school or the program, the option always is open to transfer, although not always without penalty--such as the possible loss of scholarship and/or one year of ineligibility. This approach tends to focus on the athletes as the focal point of the recruiting process.

Coaches who take this approach are not entirely cynical. In some cases, where the fit was poor between the school and the individual athlete, coaches have signed releases, recommended a particular school to attend, worked actively to get the athlete admitted, and obtain a scholarship. Such efforts may lose the current freshmen, but over time will gain support within the swimming community.

"Selling the family."-Other coaches focus on convincing the parents that the school and the program are ideally suited for the student-athlete. Since the parents have a vested interest in their child's future and in many cases have expended a great amount of time and a lot of money in supporting a swimming career,[3] they are fairly well-informed on the relative strengths and weaknesses of various swim programs. Coaches who cater to parents generally take a posture of providing information freely and openly. Conversations with coaches on recruiting suggest that the most influential persons in shaping a recruit's decision to attend a school are the parents. In some cases high school coaches and age-group coaches play a role. Less important are girl friends or former team mates who swim in the program.

Let the program speak for itself.-Some coaches let the merits of the program do the selling. "Blue chippers" often use the national rankings to determine which schools they will consider or not. Some recruits on visits have claimed they would not go to a school unless it was ranked in the top 5, or 10 by the end of the season. Clearly swimmers standards for deciding on which school to bless with their presence vary. Conversely, some "blue chippers" want to be the star on a team which is developing rather than one elite performer among many.

Top-ranked programs in institutions with reputations for academic excellence and with scholarships usually have a number of applicants from which to choose. Instead of facing the task of enticing someone to attend the school, these coaches contend with the problem of losing good athletes because of poor grades or low test scores.

Roundy and Roh (1973) surveyed top prospects in basketball in order to ascertain what influenced recruiting decisions. They found that recruits were drawn to a program by the reputation of the coaching staff; the tradition of the school in the sport; its educational opportunities; the style of play; the school's location; the quality of the facilities; parental influences; job opportunities during the summers and after graduation; and, conference prestige.

Students first? Athletes first?-The coach must decide whether to recruit athletes who can thrive intellectually at the institution, can merely survive, or surely will flunk out. If a coach repeatedly recruits good athletes, but marginal students, then the team may do well each year yet suffer high rates of turnover. This strategy may ensure a good win and loss record, but in the long-term is probably counterproductive to the development of a solid program. Most coaches would like to be able to plan on the contribution of swimmers for their full term of eligibility. In programs with high turnover caused by academic failure recruits who are weak run a high risk of not finishing their degrees. If this kind of pattern persists, the coach and the program may develop a reputation in the swimming community for exploiting athletes, a fact that can be used by other program in "negative recruiting." When a student visits a rival institution, the coach and swimmers delight in detailing the weaknesses and problems with the other's program. A coach with a reputation for exploiting athletes eventually will not be able to recruit competitively with other institutions of similar academic standing.

If a coach recruits athletes who run into academic difficulties but survive and eventually graduate, then weak students are less likely to become an issue. If the drain on resources is high in order to ensure that weaker students eventually graduate, then questions may be asked by the administration or AD about the excessive levels of financial support needed to maintain athletes for more than four years. Similarly, it does not make sense to recruit high risk students who cannot meet the basic requirements spelled out in Proposition #48.

Given the pressure in intercollegiate athletics to upgrade academics and reduce the exploitation of athletes, a coach runs a higher risk when recruiting weak students. Fortunately, the problem in swimming is not as great as in football or basketball. Historically, swimming is a sport which drew disproportionately from the middle and upper middle income groups, strata with higher proportions of better students.

There usually is a sufficient supply of good students who are "blue chippers" or "pale blue chippers" so that a coach can recruit without fears of non-compliance with Proposition #48. Many coaches have adopted the attitude of recruiting students with GPAs of 3.00 or better and solid ACT and SAT scores. These coaches argue that strong students will face a period of adjustment and may underachieve in the beginning of the freshman year until they adjust to pressures of studies, sport, and social life. By recruiting stronger students, in effect, coaches hedge their bets, by reducing the likelihood of a number of swimmers developing academic problems. Better students, if they do experience academic problems, may only drop to Cs and Bs. If coaches recruit strong students, problems of grade fixing, changes in transcripts, and extended financial assistance are virtually eliminated. Coaches should recognize that recruitment is a time consuming task with absolutely no guarantees of success.

International, national, or local?-Coaches who wish to be competitive have to decide from which pool of athletes they will draw in the recruiting process. Some coaches who have been athletes or coaches on national teams and have international visibility, or have overseas connections, or simply decide to recruit overseas, have recruited a number of foreign swimmers and divers. There are some distinct advantages in following this path. First, many foreign countries follow an elite approach to education. Often athletes, by their country's standards, may be marginal students academically and find it difficult to attend an institution of higher learning. Given the emphasis on mass education in the United States, this same athlete may be well qualified to attend an American college or university. These students are enthusiastic recruits and if given the opportunity to go to college often prove to be excellent students as well as fine athletes.

Second, it is often cheaper to recruit foreign athletes. Overseas phone calls are less expensive than paying for transportation of U.S. athletes to visit the campus. Sometimes the coach meets the foreign athletes at an international meet and no other visit is required.

Third, foreign athletes may be used to build a competitive program quickly. In track and field, several programs have moved from obscurity to national prominence by recruiting foreign athletes. The same is

true in hockey.   Some swim programs also have improved
their fortunes.

There also are some disadvantages. First, a team
with a number of foreign athletes may get stereotyped
as a program preferring foreigners to U.S. citizens.
There is a feeling among some coaches that they should
train US athletes in preparation for the next Olympics,
not foreign athletes who will compete against the
United States. Countries with ideologies and social
policies that diverge from those of the United States
sometimes are seen as "unacceptable" pools from which
to recruit athletes (Lapchick 1986). Some commentators
and coaches hold that it is inappropriate to use sport
to subsidize "undesirable" social practices. Countries
that use sport to promulgate their point of view should
be forced to pay a price. If exacting that price means
penalizing athletes, so be it. Other coaches believe
that sport and politics should be separate. Which
stance a coach takes on these issues probably depends
on whether one sees sport as (1) entirely distinct from
the pressures found in other spheres of daily life or
(2) a mirror of other spheres of social life, but in
microcosm.

Second, in some sections of the United States
there is a feeling among many people that if the
community or the state financially supports the
institution, then the sports program should represent
that constituency, not a bunch of foreigners.

The program that relies too heavily on foreigners
often becomes a target for negative recruiting. Some
odd stereotypes develop--a team with foreign athletes
is accused of needing a bunch of interpreters to run
practices. In actuality, if a student has attained an
acceptable TOEFL score and adequate grades in core
courses, then the command of English will be good
enough not only to survive academically, but surely
strong enough to get through practices.

One problem that sometimes occurs when a coach
relies on foreign athletes is that competitions to
qualify for their home country's national team may
conflict with important collegiate or university dual
meets or conference meets or possibly the NCAA
championships. When top flight swimmers and divers
suddenly leave at a critical point in the season the
team's fortunes are dramatically altered.

Today coaches are expected to recruit from across
the country if they want to build a nationally

competitive program. There no longer is as much reluctance to recruit outside a state or region in building a competitive program as there once was.

Coaches who recruit heavily from the region served by the school are heavily dependent on the quality of the programs in the area. Where strong age-group programs are found, good collegiate programs can be constructed with enthusiastic recruiting. Where programs are weak, the coach should recognize that building a top-flight program is at best difficult.

Just as recruiting international swimmers works by establishing visibility, the same phenomenon works when recruiting within the region. Coaches should attend not only the NJOs, YMCA Nationals, and invitational meets, but should also send representatives to regional age-group meets and state high school championships.

Types of athlete desired.-Coaches differ in the kinds of athletes they recruit. Some coaches emphasize a fit in personalities. They will not tender an offer to an athlete unless rapport is easily established. Some coaches feel that recruits should be able to fit into the existing structure of the team. Sometimes the coach permits the team to "blackball" a recruit; or sometimes the coach merely takes the team's sentiment as one more piece of information in the process of evaluation. Other coaches do not care about the fit as much as they do the issue of talent. Can the athlete contribute to the program? If so, how? Weak spots in the team's roster by stroke and distance must be filled. Changes in scoring of championship meets and dual meets, as well as adding or dropping events from the list in meets, change strategies required in building a team. For example, a few years ago women's swimming had a number of 50 yard sprints for fly, back, breast and a 100 individual medley. When these were deleted from the meet program it was no longer a sound strategy to recruit short distance sprinters. Longer distances became important. More recently, the change in scoring from three places to six places placed far greater emphasis on team depth in dual competition. In fact, the emphasis placed on recruiting for depth was so great that coaches recently voted to allow coaches to agreed on which scoring method to use in dual meets.

Some coaches search for athletes rather than just a swimmer or diver, under the assumption that the all-around athlete has greater potential versatility. Along the same lines, some coaches recruit swimmers who are strong in a variety of events rather than specialists.

Some coaches look for swimmers who can blend into a structured program and do not demand individualized workouts. Often it is difficult to work with "free spirits" and "prima donnas." Such individuals may be fine athletes, but coaches often feel that the costs of keeping them happy are too great. Other coaches prefer working with the less regimented athlete. They like the challenge of exchanging ideas and hammering through to a mutually agreed upon understanding of what goals are and how to best achieve them.

Earlier in Chapter 5 it was noted in passing that the coach should be sensitive to his/her mode of decision-making as well as how compatible and comfortable an athlete will be working with a particular kind of program. A coach who is autocratic and a dominant force in interpersonal interaction may overwhelm an athlete with a personality that seeks autonomy and flexibility. Conversely, a coach who is consultative and participative in style may be perceived as weak or incompetent by an athlete with a personality needing a lot of structure. If a mismatch occurs, there is the chance that the coach will make a "recruiting mistake." The athlete's performance may suffer due to frustration and unhappiness with the coach, the program, and personal performance.[4]

To be successful the program does not require that each and every swimmer be highly compatible with the head coach. A coach can recruit athletes with a range of personality types. All that is required is that the athletes feel comfortable with the coach and the coaching staff (Lanning 1979: 262-267).

In adding staff, head coaches should be sensitive to the mix of personalities between assistants and the head coach. The head coach sets the tone of the program in the mode of decision-making, in the rules that are explicitly stated and implicitly understood, and in the appropriate ways to accomplish individual and team goals. The head coach should try to hire staff members who have personality characteristics and teaching behaviors that not only compliment those of the head coach, but also provide a wider range of styles. By providing a mix of personalities, swimmers may identify which individual among the coaching staff that they feel comfortable with and feel free to engage in acts of self-disclosure--talking about personal problems beyond the tasks associated with swimming. If the head coach hires a staff with personalities identical to that of the head coach, then swimmers must get along with that personality type or leave. Some head coaches who are sensitive to this issue will select assistant coaches to play out certain roles during the year. One assistant will be the "good guy" (easy to talk too, supportive, and positive reinforcer of appropriate behaviors). Another assistant will be the task-master, a surrogate disciplinarian assigned to malingerers, hard cases, or the "criminal element" on the team. By providing choices of personality style among the assistant coaches, attention is drawn away from the head coach when swimmers have personal problems. The head coach can act as a confessor or arbiter with detachment and relatively low risk of embroilment in the daily round of hassles between assistants and swimmers.

Summary

--Recruiting is the lifeblood on the program. The basic steps involve ascertaining who is available and how good they are. To do this organizational sources and informal networks are used to generate a list of potential athletes. This list is screened to determine who is eligible academically and athletically. Student-athletes are contacted; those who are interested are contacted regularly by mail, newsletter, and phone. Top athletes are asked to visit the campus. When the signing date arrives, coaches try to get athletes to sign contracts on scholarships tendered.

--Strategies of recruiting used by coaches vary. Some believe that its is best to sell the athlete on the school and program. Some coaches assume that it is best to sell the family instead of the athlete. Others contend that it is best to let the program sell itself.

--Coaches differ as to the types of athletes recruited. Some try and recruit students first, athletes second, to reduce potential problems of grades, ineligibility, and high attrition. Others go after top-flight athletes and do not worry over grades. Some coaches recruit foreigners, others recruit nationally or regionally.

--Regardless of the type of athlete sought, compatibility between coach and athlete as well as between athletes and coaching staff are paramount for a program to be stable and successful.

REVIEW QUESTIONS

1. Identify the steps involved in the recruiting process.

2. Assume that you are responsible for organizing the recruitment process at your school. Assess the overall stature of your athletic and academic programs (review issues identified in Chapter 3), then outline the steps you would take to complete the task. As part of this exercise develop a questionnaire to send to swimmers and divers, write sample letters for contacting coaches and recruits, identify those individuals on campus that recruits will need to meet, organize the file structure for storing records on recruits, and write sample newsletters.

3. Which strategy of recruiting would you use--sell the athlete, sell the family, or let the program speak for itself? Defend your choice.

4. In recruiting your team would you emphasize scholarship or athletic ability? Provide a justification for your position.

5. Would you recruit internationally, nationally, or locally?

NOTES

[1] It is important to identify the number of swimmers and divers who will not return. Among those not returning, those with and without scholarships must be counted. This information is needed in calculating budgets costs associated with recruiting, travel for athletes visiting the school, as well as junkets for coaches to visit and scout. Those athletes who leave create gaps in the lineup that must be filled. Knowing the number of positions open gives the coach a rough idea of how much time and energy will be needed to build a large enough pool of recruits to ensure a solid roster for next year.

[2] The analogy of the wedding cake is taken from criminology. It was originally set forth by Friedman and Percival (1981).

[3] In some cases the expenses for supporting a swimmer or diver with fees for training facilities, clinics, summer camps, lessons, equipment, entry fees, travel, and other various and sundry items cost more than the total scholarship package for four years. It is not surprising that parents are interested.

[4] One strategy to follow to improve the chance of a fit between athlete, school, and swimming program is to prepare a set of answers to questions posed by Wadley (1986). Bill Wadley identifies key questions athletes should ask of a college swimming program when searching for a school to attend. Not only would the answers be useful to the athlete and parents, but preparing the answers would cause the coach to reflect on those aspects of the program often taken for granted.

"Tell me, dear, how did your day go?"
"I don't know. Some days it seems like everyone wants a piece of my hide. The first thing this morning the AD calls me with a request to double check on illegal booster contacts with the kids. No sooner do I get off the phone that in walks the SID and she wants to set up an afternoon appointment for photographs. We decided on Tuesday afternoon. I had to call Dr. George because he told one of the swimmers to stay out of the water for 10 days due to a high white cell count. The count should be high; the kids have been averaging 16000 to 18000 meters a day this week. The trainer called with a list of swimmers who reported with complaints of sore shoulders. The academic advisor phoned to warn me that three of my best kids are cutting classes in English and are depending on boyfriends to take notes. The secretary wants to take off next week. Campus security wants to interview the gals concerning the break-in to the team room and rifling of the lockers. ASCA send a letter for dues. At least the NCAA and parents haven't called today."

****

The coach is a social actor involved in a variety of social relationships. These relationships involve not only individuals inside the sport community, but those outside of it as well.

Head coach and key people

Athletic department personnel.-Within the sport community the coach's role definitions and performances are examined in interaction with the individuals inside the athletic department and outside of it. Those inside include the athletic director, sports information representatives, team physician, trainer, aquatics director, academic advisor, secretarial and janitorial staff, representatives from food and housing services, and campus security.

1. Athletic Director.-Membership in the sports community does not guarantee general knowledge across all sports. Interests tend to be limited to a specific sport or a few sports. Athletic directors often are presumed to be conversant about all sports.

Often, however, an AD has only coached in one particular sport, so while serving as the AD must develop an understanding of and appreciation for the problems faced by coaches in other sports. The coaches often have to spend time in making sure that an open style of communication is fostered between themselves and the AD. Coaches who presume that ADs are familiar with problems confronted in administering a swimming program--when they are not--will meet with frustration. Coaches will presume messages have been sent and understood, although clarity has yet to be achieved. The rationale for requests may be patently obvious to coaches, yet a mystery to the AD.

An assessment of how well-informed the AD is regarding swimming can be gleaned from conversations held during the interview process and after joining the staff. Just as the AD is sensitive to the coach's use of language when discussing coaching and sport, the coach must listen carefully to the vocabulary used by the AD when discussing the goals and the structure of the swimming program. If the AD invokes the proper vocabulary, conveys a rudimentary knowledge of the organizational needs of swimming programs, and an openness to learn, then the conversations between coach and AD will be more productive than in a situation where the AD has a favorite sport or combination of sports and is reticent to master new spheres of knowledge. Answers by the AD to the coach's questions will contribute to an understanding of the coach's job description, the nature of interaction expected between AD and coach, the arrangement of responsibilities within the athletic department, and the overall place of athletics and swimming within the college or university.

The head coach probably will not appreciate the full range of responsibilities that an AD must face. The head coach tends to become "nearsighted," focusing on the needs of the swimming program to the exclusion of other teams and the athletic department in general. It is mandatory that the head coach be open and try to comprehend the pressures that face the AD, particularly as each sport hosts its events during the course of the season. It is not unusual for the AD at some point during the year to oversee the hosting of one, two, or possibly three conference championships. Add to these duties the tasks of directing a job search for a coaching vacancy, deliberating over disciplinary actions for athletes on various squads, serving on university committees, attending NCAA meetings, and preparing the annual budget, and then one begins to develop a feel for the pressures exerted on the AD's time and energy-level.

The nature of the interaction between AD and coach is fixed by the formal constraints of the jobs, not personalities. A coach should remember that job tenure is linked to performance, not friendship. An AD is the caretaker of the entire athletic department. Either a coach or a program may be expendable, if circumstances warrant. Job security and respect accrue based on one's record of achievement. Where a proven record exists, there is greater tolerance for the "off" year. Latitude is permitted when it is necessary to rebuild. Where no history of success has been established there is a tendency to remove the coach and begin anew. Coaches should recognize that the "fastest gun" in the athletic department is always the AD.

2. Sports information office and media.-More often than not exchanges between swimming team staff and media are limited to the head coach. Other staff members may be interviewed if a request is cleared with the head coach. In most universities and colleges with highly competitive programs, there is a sports information director(SID) or a member of the athletic department staff who deals with the media on a regular basis.

At the beginning of every season, each athlete and member of the coaching staff is asked to fill out a questionnaire providing biographical data, information on sports career--outstanding accomplishments (member of the Olympic team, national team), outstanding performances (world, national, conference, or school record), personal best performances for events swum in meters and yards, honors received--hobbies, major, current interests, and reasons for attending the institution. Any time a member of the media wishes to interview an athlete or coach, the sports information director or representative can reach into the file and extract information to be used as "color" in supplementing the information obtained in the interview. At the beginning of each season, the sports information office requests that a practice session be devoted to taking photographs for the SID's office. Individual portraits (full-length and head shot), class group shots, team shots, and some action shots are snapped. Two series of photos are typically run. First, shots are taken in team meet "warmups." Second, shots are taken while athletes are dressed up--women in dresses and men in suits. These photographs are used throughout the year. They are part of the team promotional pamphlet used for recruiting, which is usually made available at meets on the media display table. Photos also are sent to the newspaper and television when feature stories, exclusives, or color spots are run.

Institutions with a sports information office prefer to have requests for interviews, either with a coach or an athlete, channeled through and cleared by the SI office. Foreknowledge of interviews prevents surprises from appearing in the press--such as charges of racism, brutality, or sexual harassment; reports of personal conflicts, claims of grade fixing; and, charges of illegal booster gifts.

Foreknowledge permits the SID to work with the coaching staff to emphasize particular themes, events, or personalities that the athletic department may be highlighting in a given season or year. For instance, football may push a player for the Heisman trophy award; basketball may be eyeing a spot with the Final Four; and swimming may have a few former Olympians. Each program should be touted to enhance its visibility and the overall reputation of the athletic department.

In some schools, athletic departments conduct seminars and videotape practice press interviews to teach staff and athletes how to respond to questions in order to present themselves and the institution in the most favorable possible light. Helpful comments on posture, speech patterns to avoid, and use of proper diction and syntax go a long way to upgrade the image of the coach and the athlete with the television audience. Nothing is worse for the image of the program than inarticulate, camera-shy coaches and athletes.

Most typically, media representatives want to talk with the coach at the beginning of the season. They want to find out what kinds of performances are anticipated from the team and from key individuals; what regular season meets may be of interest (rivalries); what invitational, national, and international meets may be scheduled for the team; or what the possible trips are for elite performers. When the program has an athlete, either with extraordinary ability or an unusual background, this person becomes an obvious choice for a "color spot" on the local sports news.

The media also is receptive to reports on meet results. The SID or SI representative may be assigned to phone in the results of meets to various newspapers and television stations that serve an audience with an interest in the school. Each newspaper has a sports desk with a specific individual assigned to cover designated sports. Similarly, television stations have individuals assigned to particular sports. In some cases the newspaper will pay a nominal fee to the coach or the athletic department for calling in results of athletic contests. Most newspapers in recent years have adopted a sports summary page that includes results of games, track and field meets, swim meets, auto races, and so forth.

If the sports information office does not provide a representative to cover swimming, then the responsibility for contacting the media usually falls on the coach. The head coach may call in the results or delegate the responsibility to an assistant coach or manager. Whoever calls should ask what format is used to report the meet results so that they are easy to transcribe during dictation. The person assigned to call in the meet results should keep a list of phone numbers and names for each of the media representatives to be contacted. After the results have been dictated and transcribed, the desk person often asks for comments on the team's performance or on some outstanding feat. The head coach should decide before talking to the media which aspects of the meet or team's performance wishes to highlight. These responses often appear as unedited copy on the sports page.

If the head coach wants coverage for the team's activities, then the coach should take time to develop a working relationship with representatives of the local television and newspapers. When sportswriters cover an event, the coach should take time to talk with them. The coach should find out what kinds of stories the editors like to print, broadcast, or televise. The coach should learn what kinds of statements can be made that are quotable in a favorable light, and what kinds of statements make "good copy" at the expense of the athlete, the coach, or the institution. The coach should always practice "newsthink," pre-censoring what is said to avoid surprises.

In any sport there are numerous horror stories of items that appeared in print or on the air in which statements were taken out of context, distorted, or misquoted. Inevitably such a story either embarrasses a coach, team, athlete, or administrator; repercussions always prove to be most unpleasant. Efforts to exact a retraction or clarification only compound the problem. In some cases the story maligns the rival with the unfortunate consequence of "psyching them" for the "big game" and resulting in one's own defeat. Although fixing a causal connection between the appearance of media story and defeat is dicey, the association presumably occurs enough times to warrant caution when dealing with the press.[1]

Some swim coaches like to deal with the media directly rather than letting sports information representatives file stories. They feel that the press is more likely to give priority to the money-making sports like football, basketball, baseball, and hockey. To counteract this tendency the coach acts as an advocate for the program. Assertiveness increases the likelihood of swimming coverage. The coach must contact the press with sufficient advance time to allow editors to schedule a release. Even if an interview is on file, an editor faced with a deadline and a crowded sports schedule, if forced to choose between a money-making sport and swimming, will not pick swimming.

If an event or story is important and the coach wants to get adequate coverage, one method is to divide the story into parts and submit multiple releases. The coach should time the releases to build interest in the event starting three to four weeks ahead of time (Boesch 1977: 19-31).

One way to ensure coverage of swimming is to get the local newspaper to select an all-conference swimming and diving team for each year. A first, second, or honorable mention team and the top swimming and diving coaches for the year can be picked by either the sportswriters or voted on by the coaches. This strategy accomplishes at least two purposes. First, it honors the outstanding performances of coaches and athletes. Second, it provides the newspaper with materials to use in anticipation of the conference meet each year by highlighting returning athletes and comparing the present generation of athletes with past generations. Any items that can be pulled from morgue files will make the sportswriter's job easier when covering swimming.

The problems confronted in dealing with the local press often are multiplied when dealing with a campus newspaper. Count the inches devoted to swimming, a year-round sport, versus a major sport, and the pattern of bias found in the local press is repeated. Some coaches who have swimmers who are dating campus newspaper personnel have exploited this opportunity to gain coverage. (Incidentally, women's sports generally receive less coverage than men's sports. Women's coaches have to fight the double battle of being mentors in a minor sport and victims of sexism.)

A head coach who wants to increase the amount of coverage and visibility for swimming sometimes has to add elements of "display" to meets to stimulate spectator interest and attendance (Stone 1955). (See discussion on student booster groups at The University of Tennessee.)

The coach, when meeting with media representatives, should be sensitive to the different perspectives from which each operates. The coach's orientation focuses on doing what is best for the performance of the team, conducting a smoothly-run meet and minimizing any expenditures of energy by the athletes. The media people's orientation is promotion, entertainment, fan appeal, and excitement and sales--in a word, marketability. (For a list of factors on which coaches and promotional representatives differ, see Freas 1980: 155-156.)

Most importantly, when the SID or SI representative and personnel from the local media do a good job of reporting, the coach should call them and thank them for their assistance. Let them know their coverage increased interest in or attendance at the event or meet.

3. Physician.-The head coach may be fortunate to have a team physician who has specialized in sportsmedicine, or who by virtue of prolonged association with the athletic program, has developed an understanding of many of the problems confronted when trying to keep athletes in training and ready for competition. Perhaps a physician is not familiar with the sport-specific side effects resulting from intensive training to increase aerobic and anaerobic capacities. For instance, heavy doses of mileage may lead to tissue damage which in turn may cause elevated white blood cell counts. An above normal white blood cell count is one of the symptoms associated with exhaustion and mononucleosis often found among college patients. Swimmers may also suffer shoulder and knee injuries given the highly repetitive nature of arm and leg movement in training. Swimmers may develop eye, skin, and teeth problems due to long exposure to chlorinated water. Failure of the physician to recognize these symptoms leads the coach to question

115

the physician's expertise. Coaches dislike it when the physician prescribes rest for a period that is perceived by the coach as "too long." Although it is aggravating to lose swimmers from training sessions or from competition when injuries occur, to lose them due to an alleged misdiagnosis is frustrating. Any time the coach has a team that is short-handed, whether in practice or a meet, it is frustrating and increases stress.

Coaches, in order to develop an open and supporting relationship with the team physician, may engage in a professional exchange of information on research findings in sports medicine and discuss their respective role demands in working with athletes. Journals in medicine, physical education and fitness, and general health should be checked regularly for items of interest. Offprints or photo copies of current articles should be circulated among members of the medical staff, training staff, and coaching staff.[2]

4. Trainer.-At the beginning of each year, the trainer meets with the team to review policies on reporting and treatment of injuries, procedures to follow when involved in therapy, and guidelines covering drug tests. Typically, injuries and complaints are first screened by the trainer. In cases where the symptoms warrant, the trainer will arrange an appointment with the physician. Should the case require a trip to the emergency room, arrangements will be made. In all cases the trainer checks with the coach to report on the status of the athlete. A written statement is shown to the coach designating treatment and therapy, is returned to the trainer, and filed. Athletes who are injured and for whom a recuperative therapy is prescribed are expected to meet with the trainer and follow that regimen. Failure to do so is grounds for disciplinary action.[3]

Schools' policies on informing athletes of the procedures followed in testing for NCAA banned drugs vary. When the tests are administered (as part of pre-season physical, randomly, before contests, or when performances suggest a possible problem) also differ across institutions. Which tests are run (testing for the complete spectrum of NCAA banned drugs, recreational drugs, or selected drugs) depend on the sport and vary by program. How the results are handled (as a medical report or a disciplinary problem) also differ. The courses of action taken when positive results are obtained (probation, suspension, loss of privileges or scholarship, dismissal from the team or school) show variation by programs. Whatever the procedures are for the institution, all parties concerned must have a clear and complete knowledge of them.

Over the years, the coach learns to expect an increase in physical complaints at certain points in the academic calendar and the season. As the first wave of examinations, term papers, and reports come due, there are complaints of stomach upset, sore throats, low-grade fevers, and headaches. This same pattern is repeated during the week of final exams. Similarly, as the pressure of training is increased (moving from one practice to two practices per day) the complaints of sore shoulders, knees, backs, and so forth crop up. During peak periods of intensive training, symptoms associated with physical exhaustion and fatigue also are reported. All complaints must be checked. During these periods the trainer and coach get to know one another very well. Athletes who repeatedly claim to have symptoms simply may not be able to cope with stress. Some may worry about grades more than swimming, thus try to avoid swimming in order to study. A few may be hypochondriacs[4] or malingerers.

Two problems that often occur on women's swimming teams, from age-group through college, are <u>bulimia</u> and <u>anorexia nervosa</u>. Coaches often encourage swimmers and divers to avoid excessive body fat and to try to increase muscle. Among athletes with strong achievement motivations, some often eschew appropriate nutritional habits and exercise as acceptable means for weight loss, but resort to inappropriate methods. Coaches must learn to recognize the clinical symptoms and behavioral clues associated with these disorders, then must refer the athletes to the appropriate professionals for help (Dummer et al. 1986).

    5. Aquatics Director.-In many schools the head coach is responsible for both the men's and women's programs and is also the Aquatics Director. In this situation the coach has the advantage of fixing the agenda for practices and meets with a minimum of fuss. But when the coach does not operate in a joint capacity, an Aquatics Director schedules pool time, use of equipment, and physical plant. The head coach must recognize the priorities given to the various uses of facilities for instruction, students and faculty recreation, community programs, and competitive swimming. The relative mix of pressures in scheduling, as well as any favoritism of men over women and vice versa, establishes the boundaries within which requests

may be made. Whenever a site is open for multiple uses, the head coach has to play the dual role of advocate and negotiator in order to protect the interests of his/her program. Incidentally, one of the strategies administrators may employ either to support or constrain the power of the head coach is to redefine who has the ultimate responsibility for scheduling the use of facilities.[5]

      6. Academic Advisor.-In recent years many athletic departments or schools have created the position of academic advisor to ensure the individual is a student as well as an athlete. The creation of this position is a reaction by administrators, faculty, and ADs to the charges of institutional exploitation of athletes without the concomitant concern for the athlete's academic development and general well-being in life after sport. Typically advisors check athletes' schedules; help with registration; line up tutors for athletes with problems; handle the ordering of athletic department books to loan students during the quarter; oversee study hall, keep academic files on grades, declared major, and progress in major; double check the athlete's eligibility under school, conference, and/or NCAA rules; and check with faculty on athletes' attendance, performance, and needs.

     Where such a position is available, the head coach needs to keep abreast of services provided by the advisor and the schedule of activities required of student-athletes. Coaches react variously to academic advisors. If the AD strongly backs academics, then the advisor is taken seriously. If the advisor is a graduate assistant and the position turns over every two years, then the coach who has been in the institution for some time probably feels more knowledgeable than the advisor and treats the position lightly. Whether the coach supports the position becomes a matter of whim. The academic background of the athletes also affects the coach's reaction to the position. Where athletes are strong academically and are able to take responsibility for planning their own curricula, the coach will be less sympathetic to the role of the advisor and rely less on the service. Where there are academic problems, a relationship between coach and academic advisor often is strengthened. In short, the nature of the ties is set by the tone of the institution, the AD, and the whims of the coach (see Monaghan 1955: 37 & 39).

      7. Secretarial staff.-Coaches rely directly on departmental secretaries for assistance and support

in handling mail, messages, processing budget requests, and a variety of other activities necessary for the survival of the program. If the head coach or assistant coaches who interact with the secretarial staff create bad feelings, priorities given to swimming program projects by the secretarial staff may be subtly altered. Information needed from secretaries to complete tasks accurately and on time may not be volunteered, but extracted only by direct questioning (difficult if one the coach is new or unfamiliar with the administrative procedures of an institution). Conversely, when good relationships exist between the coaching staff and the support staff, the latter's actions are valuable in organizing and expediting athletic department functions and competitive events.

8. Janitorial staff.-The head coach and the assistant coaches also need to develop good working relationships with the janitorial staff. Adjustments in use of the pool--both practice time and lane use-- may occasionally be required in order to clean the pool and install, replace, or fix equipment. Civility and an occasional "coffee and doughnut" run early in the morning often ensure that requests for service will be cheerfully completed.

The head coach who fails to understand that work slow-downs, "lost" job requests, and disclaimers of tasks falling outside of the job description, are strategies easily used in retaliation for snubs or discourtesies. An insensitive coach may wait a long time before work is done.

9. Food services and student housing.-How room and board are administered differs from campus to campus. Generally, at the beginning of each academic year all students on campus are expected to inform the food services program whether they intend to participate in the meal plan contract program or not. Those swimmers who participate must indicate which contract (how many meals per week) they intend to sign. Scholarship swimmers who receive food as part or all of their scholarship allocation must inform the coach of their intentions. Similarly, students who intend to live in university housing are expected to inform housing program officials and sign contacts.

Requests for roommates must be submitted when housing contracts are signed. Again, scholarship athletes who receive room must confirm rooming assignments so that the coach can account for total scholarships assigned. The head coach should know

119

which officials in each of these offices to contact should questions arise over meal and housing contracts.

Occasionally the head coach may need to make use of university food services to provide foods for various social gatherings. The coach should learn the procedures for ordering meals, for making arrangements for setting up venues where meals will be served, and for billing payment of services.

10. Campus security.-From time to time it is necessary to contact campus security personnel to arrange for parking passes for parents of swimmers, visitors, meet officials, visiting teams, and dignitaries. The head coach should know which member of the campus police force is in charge of handling parking privileges.

Sometimes security is needed to prevent gate crashers from entering a competition site without proper identification. The head coach may have to set up a system of identification and passes for admission to events by coaches, competitors, press, and spectators. These procedures must be coordinated with the AD, SID, and campus security.

It is a good policy to warn visitors and incoming teams that college campuses are not havens, free from crime. Visiting coaches should be forewarned that they are responsible for team equipment, towels, banners, and so forth. Should theft occur (team warmup suits and banners are prime targets), theft reports need to be filed and the appropriate authorities informed. Whenever an event is scheduled, a member of the coaching staff should be sure to notify the campus police well in advance so they can schedule personnel to cover the venue.

Other insiders within the sports community.-Individuals outside the athletic department who are members of the sports community but with whom the coach must interact include other coaches and the adult and student boosters and fans.

1. Other coaches.-History and personality shape the relationships between rival coaches. A coach who is amiable and easy-going, who acts as a gracious host when others visit, and who maintains control with dignity, probably will easily establish rapport with other coaches. Conversely, a coach who is driven by the desire to win at all costs, or who engages in artifices calculated to upset competitors and

negatively affect performance, who is egotistically after rankings will be held at some distance by other coaches.

A coach's style often influences meet strategies. A coach with a superior team competing against another coach with a good reputation may decide to "hold back" instead of running up the score. The coach may let swimmers compete in off-events or designate certain swimmers as exhibition (and thus not score). Both actions tend to keep the score down.

Conversely, a coach competing against another targeted for retribution for previous grievances, given the opportunity will allow the score to become lopsided. Numerous strategies will be tried over the years to garner those "sweet victories of retribution." Coaches who have been active for a number of years, experiencing good years with top talent and lean years with little, have diaries filled with grievances, real or imagined, to redress. In some cases the feelings are so strongly held that coaches refuse to schedule one another, and only compete at conference championships or NCAA meets. Relationships between antagonists tend to be formal and businesslike.

Coaches differ in their willingness to pass on their knowledge and insights to others. Some coaches are secretive, claiming they learned their lessons without any guidance. They claim that others should do the same. "After all, if I pass secrets on to others, they only will be used against me."

Some coaches are open and freely share their knowledge. They see the profession as growing and maturing with refinement of principles and techniques. "If I can be of benefit to someone, all are enriched."

How secretive or altruistic the coach often depends on whether the questioner is an assistant or an outsider. Coaches generally view loyalty as an extremely important trait. Many errors of omission and commission will be tolerated, but failure to support the coach--either by withholding support, adopting a neutral stance on issues, or participating in a "palace revolution"--are grounds for dismissal.

Assistant coaches must take heed that evaluations of performance and letters of recommendation play an important part in moving to another job. After all, assistant coaches should recognize that their professional future may be tied to their ability to

<u>network</u> or use the head coach's network. (The term means (1) the development of social bonds among individuals who share common or like interests; and (2) the use of social ties to obtain some social end.) In any job an individual builds a number of contacts, acquaintances, and friendships. How individuals are perceived by their contacts[6] may shape their ability to move from one job to another. An assistant who fosters dissention no doubt will get a poor recommendation.

2. Adult boosters and fans.-Over the years the NCAA, partly at the prompting of coaches and partly at the request of ADs, has moved increasingly to circumscribe the activities of boosters interacting with athletes. (For a definition of **booster** consult the <u>NCAA Manual</u> 1985-86: 17-18.) Conversations with boosters inevitably turn back to the "good old" days when the NCAA took less interest in the affairs of boosters, or at least allowed greater latitude in their actions. Under the old regime, boosters say they could get to know the coaches, athletes, and support staff of the various sports programs better. They contend that booster-sponsored activities--such as setting up foster parents for athletes, taking athletes out for birthdays, and allowing athletes to visit in their homes--provided a social support system for the athletes that has since been stripped away. They believe that these activities provided the athletes with social ties to replace social bonds severed when the athletes moved away from home. They claim they provided a social network--beyond the school and team environment--athletes to turn to when problems arose with studies, faculty, friends, or the coaches. They believe that these kinds of activities kept a number of athletes in school who might have dropped out without such third party social support. They argue that the benefits of such a system far outweighed any abuses that might have operated.

Boosters also claim that it is more fun to follow the teams when you know the athletes personally rather than see them as merely names on a roster. Similarly, it is easier to support a program when you know the coaching staff and they know you. Such ties develop a network of potential helpers when a special event is hosted by a program or the athletic department. Severing of ties between players and boosters reduces the feelings of intimacy and identification that occur.[7] The moves by the NCAA to reduce the involvement of boosters (for fear of providing illegal inducements to athletes to attend an institution, or providing illegal benefits not available to other students, thus corrupting the sport) has unfortunately removed much of the sociability from college sport.

If the effort originated to reduce the likelihood of corruption bred by excessive favoritism, the move has at best been only marginally successful. People who are going to engage in activities such as gift giving or providing services to athletes will do so whether or not the actions are deemed illegal.

Further, by stripping away sociability, any norms of equity that might have governed gift giving in friendship relationships, such as the amount of the value of the gift, have been eliminated. The moral claims of friendship, which would have kept many excesses in check, have been removed by turning control and regulatory powers over to people outside of the relationship. As athletes become more distant from boosters, they become more like objects. Athletes are "things" to take care of like machine parts in order to keep the machine operating smoothly. The emphasis is on performance as product rather performance of individuals as people. Given this mentality, it is easy to offer goods and services to athletes: "You pay your money, you get results." Clearly either system has its excesses, but under the current set of rules, benefits are perhaps justified more readily as a form of economic exchange; conversely, under the former rules, a booster's gifts were viewed at best as acts of friendship, or perhaps as acts of paternalism.

Under current NCAA regulations, athletes and boosters, as well as coaches, may gather after contests under the mantle of potluck dinners, awards banquets, and fund-raising meetings governed by the institution. The nature of such contacts needs to be cleared by the AD or NCAA representative to ensure no violations occur. In the past contacts usually were aboveboard. However, given the stringency of NCAA regulations governing booster-athlete contacts and the fear of potentially violating rules, many boosters who used to interact with athletes now limit contacts to approved meetings, or have given up trying to contact the athletes. A few boosters continue to maintain the same old practices until they are caught. The institution attempts to protect itself against such violations, warning coaches to oversee the activities of their athletes--encouraging them to report contacts outside the regulations and limit the number of contacts with boosters. Where friendships are involved, it is difficult to legislate their elimination. The coach to protect against charges of failing to oversee the actions of athletes, should keep a file on athlete-booster interactions. In cases with even a hint of impropriety, the coach should report the incident to the AD and keep a summary on file. Where a violation occurs and involves gift giving, the institution often moves to identify the offenders, to report the case to the NCAA, and if necessary, to sever formal ties between the institution and the booster.

3. Student boosters.-In many of the larger athletic programs there is a student booster organization. It is comprised of students, non-athletes who assist with team functions--such as running swim meets, hosting recruits, assisting with clerical work, record keeping, and "hyping" the program among the student body (Bussard 1972; Armistead 1980). Some coaches set up voluntary support groups to help officiate at meets--all males for the women's team and all females for the men's team. Often these groups have colorful, eye-catching, and symbolic uniforms. For instance, Ray Bussard, Head Men's Coach at The University of Tennessee: (1) built a large wooden orange "T" through which swimmers enter before each meet; (2) instituted a student booster club called the "Timettes" of females--earlier clad in boots, cowboy hats, and orange and white uniforms, and more recently attired in orange blouses and skirts with white socks and sneakers--who serve as timers, finish judges, and assist with the scoring at the diving table; (3) started the team tradition of wearing coonskin caps, Davy Crockett style; and (4) presented the colors--held by two bikini-clad coeds in a canoe afloat in the diving well at the start of the meet (Bussard 1972).

In some schools the booster organization assists in all sports. In other schools each sport must develop its own booster organization, or the men's and the women's teams must build separate organizations. It is far more efficient to create an infra-structure to which all sports can turn for assistance, with various sub-sets of individuals identified as interested in particular teams.

In schools with a Greek system--fraternities and sororities--personnel can frequently be solicited to assist with sporting events. Various Greek memberships receive credits from the national headquarters for performing such campus service activities. If a ROTC program is available, representatives from the corp may serve, providing that they can wear a uniform or T-shirt designating organizational affiliation. Any

organization that espouses public service and wants
visibility for its efforts should be contacted and
included as part of the support system for the program.

Coaches need to court both adult and student
boosters. The coach should attend their functions, be
willing to chat with them, answer questions on the
status of athletes, the progress of the program, future
prospects, and so forth. Boosters form the backbone of
the fund-raising efforts. Booster club organizations
are one of the major sources of money for the
development fund in an athletic department's budget.
Boosters are regularly solicited by the fund-raising
officer or development office representative, the AD,
or particular coach making a pitch for money. These
funds are necessary for purchases of large equipment--
such as a electronic timing system, personal computer
and computer programs to run meets, electronic
scoreboards, public address system, Nautilus-type
equipment, and repairs to the pool and facilities, to
name but a few. In some cases if the team is asked to
attend an invitational meet or individuals are invited
to represent the school at special functions, boosters
will donate funds to the athletic department earmarked
for particular activities. Annual award banquets and
athletes' awards can be sponsored through this system
of earmarking gifts. A systematic effort is required
to build a broadly-based audience that supports the
athletic department's programs through attendance at
events, assistance with hosting events, and donating
funds. Any efforts that the coach makes to build a
support network will return dividends many fold.

4. Other teams on campus.-A head coach should
not forget to support other teams in the athletic
department. Once the athletes appear on campus and the
daily grind of training, classes, and administrative
trivia starts, it is very easy for a coach to overlook
other sports. To ensure a sense of camaraderie with
other teams, the coaches, swimmers, and divers should
attend games en masse, forming their own cheering
section. It builds team spirit and department spirit.
When teams are training over vacation breaks--Christmas
and Spring, and very few students are in town--
attending each others' contests ensures some support
rather than none. When other teams are out of season
and the coach needs help to host and produce an event,
the groundwork has been laid for possible assistance.

5. Parents.-One of the more salient social
relationships that a head coach must foster is with
parents of swimmers. This relationship may begin when

the swimmer first joins a program as an age-grouper. Parents are concerned with the children's well-being, more especially their physical development and social and psychological growth. Not only do they want their son or daughter to learn swimming skills and reach a high level of physical conditioning, they also want the son or daughter to learn a positive attitude toward sport and competition, develop a sense of self-worth, and maintain a balance between swimming, studies, and a social life. The coach must form an understanding of how each of these issues is defined by the parents and how the parents interact with the child. Once the parents' motives and actions are understood, the coach is better able to place the swimmers' action within a broader context and more easily and accurately interpret their behavior.

Similarly, the coach is better able to focus on those kinds of behaviors and problems about which the parents are particularly anxious, and must be kept informed. It is important for the coach to establish a strong bond of communication with the parents in order to elicit their support. If the parents are aware of the coach's concern for the well-being of the athlete, and are certain that the coach understands the athlete's personality, and is able to address the child's strengths and weaknesses, then the parents will be more likely to rely on the coach's judgment. In effect, the parents will feel comfortable turning their son or daughter over to a coach concerned with the best interests of the child. The coach to some extent acts as a surrogate parent.

If this kind of trust is established between coach and parent, when the child faces problems in dealing with the coach and turns to mom and dad for support, the coach usually can depend on the parents to support his/her judgment. Without the parents' support, the coach faces potential problems every time an athlete turns to them. Parents who do not support a coach can easily be persuaded to contact the athletic director or other administrators in order to protect their child's interests.

In some cases establishing a solid relationship between coach and parents may begin during the recruiting process. It is important to clearly establish program goals, philosophy of coaching, and how the program serves the physical, social, and psychological needs of the athlete. The parents' support is mandatory, if the coach expects the athlete to select the school in the first place. The community of swimming parents is a tightly knit, network. If the coach develops rapport with parents, they will freely endorse the program. Conversely, without parents' support, building a stable program is difficult.

Head coach and key organizations

For the most part, coaches attempt to adhere to rules promulgated by their conference, NCAA, and institutions.

Ties with the conference.-Most conferences at some point in the year provide an opportunity for coaches in a sport to convene in order to discuss common problems. The topics may cover such items as selecting sites for conference championships, creating of rules beyond those specified by the NCAA for the conduct of championship and dual meets, establishing parameters for the number of dual or triangle meets to be held among conference members, setting up mechanisms for speeding the flow of information between conference coaches on meet results among common opponents and each other, and obtaining more extensive and more frequent media coverage for the sport. Where there are problems in interpreting the rules, coaches seek to iron out differences, enact new rules, or at least generate agreements which guide the conduct of coaches. Where actions are required by ADs or presidents of schools, motions carried by the coaches are submitted for approval. In general, coaches' meetings provide an opportunity to discuss ways in which the sport may be improved as well as consolidate the position of the sport with the public and with the conference schools.

It is important for new coaches in the conference to participate in these sessions in order to develop an understanding of how the history of interpersonal relationships between coaches shapes conference schedules, rules, and suggested modifications in procedures. Often the differences in philosophy, the animosities, and the rivalries between coaches get played out in the actions proposed, debated, and enacted. Actions proposed often reflect attempts by a coach to gain advantage over certain opponents. Conversely, coaches sometimes band together to bring a recalcitrant member into line. Assistant coaches, as part of their apprenticeship, should be encouraged to attend and learn.

Getting along with the conference office is usually a straightforward task. Officials are available to inform the coaches on: conference policy and rules; the relative responsibilities of coaches in the reporting of information to the conference office-- such as submitting eligibility lists and copies of budgets for athletic events conducted under the aegis of conference sponsorship; and the handling of requests for trophies. Any time there are questions on policy matters or procedures, coaches can contact the office, usually by phone, and obtain answers. As a matter of form, once a coach obtains a clarification on a policy or rule interpretation it should be verified by a letter which is kept it on file.

Ties with the NCAA.-Getting along with the NCAA office is more bothersome. Coaches have to be particularly sensitive to NCAA rules and regulations. These are sufficiently numerous, and in many instances so cumbersome to administer, that care is warranted if one wants to run a clean shop.

Each year an updated NCAA Manual is given to member coaches and a subscription to NCAA News is sent to member coaches. The Manual contains a constitution, by-laws, and cases with questions and answers to guide the reader in interpreting regulations. In the NCAA News one of the sections reports on rule interpretations on cases that have been handled by the NCAA office. These interpretations are clipped and placed in the Manual in the appropriate section. Given the ever increasing body of interpretations, it is important for coaches to stay abreast of the rules and changing nature of interpretations. Coaches should recognize that if they operate on the assumption that the rules are based on common sense, or on a sense of fair play and honesty, they no doubt will commit a rule violation.

The two areas where violations of NCAA rules more frequently occur involve (1) recruiting and (2) providing athletes illegal benefits not normally extended to other students. If a coach wishes to avoid problems, the standard practice is to talk to the other experienced coaches in the athletic department and find out what they do. If qualms still exist, the coach should check with the AD or the NCAA representative. In some cases the school encourages the coach to contact the legislative service staff for an interpretation.

Sometimes coaches may violate the rules unwittingly and self-report the incident to the institution. Still other coaches religiously conform to the rules.

Coaches who know of a rule violation more likely than not will file a report and notify their AD of it. A file is then kept at the institution. Coaches generally are reluctant to self-report an action to the NCAA office. They are most reluctant to report other coaches for violations. The typical strategies are to ignore the violations, ask the other coach to desist, or in severe cases ask the other coach to self-report. In those cases where a coach has reported violations of others, there is a sentiment that, although the action was ethically necessary, they would be most hesitant to have to repeat the experience.

Ties with the ASCA.-Coaches, as part of their professional development, should join the ASCA and keep abreast of the professional literature that is disseminated to its membership. The coach who has a penchant for professing personal views in print should contribute comments and articles to the various organs available to the profession. Some coaches depict the emergence of Swimming World and Junior Swimmer as one of the most noteworthy efforts to promote the professionalism within the swimming community. Despite the reluctance, if not fear of many people to write, teaching others remains a professional goal and coaches should recognize that one article in Swimming World and Junior Swimmer reaches a wider audience than a single coach could teach in many years.

The coach should attend the annual World Clinic meetings in order to keep informed of new techniques, new ideas on organization, motivation, training, nutrition, and so forth. Participation also provides an opportunity for the coach to establish and maintain ties with others in the coaching community.

If affordable, the coach should join professional organizations in other countries to keep abreast of international swimming. It certainly helps avoid the typical American tendency toward parochialism which is occasionally demonstrated at the World Games and the Olympics.

Summary

--The head coach lives in a social world of many relationships with people inside the athletic department, with people on campus, and with people off campus. Many of the social relationships involve people inside and outside the world of sport.

--Another part of the coach's social world involves ties with officials in the conference, with NCAA officials, and with other coaches who are part of the ASCA.

REVIEW QUESTIONS

1. List the names and positions of each person in the athletic department of your alma mater, current school, or a school you know well, with whom the swim coach must interact.

2. For the same school find out what the policies of the athletic department are on: coach and athlete contacts with the media; reporting and treatment of illnesses and injuries; drug testing and drug violations; handling academic counseling; and working with booster organizations.

3. Talk with a coach and find out the kinds of rivalries that exist between coaches and how these influence meet scheduling and preparation.

4. Review the discussion of leadership styles in Chapter 5 and then describe which approach you would use in dealing with each of the parties discussed in this chapter.

NOTES

[1]   Given the number of teams and media reports presented for each team, the actual probabilities of a single story significantly affecting an athlete's or a team's performance are extremely small.   Anecdotal evidence tends to be exaggerated. It makes good copy. It is easy to blame the press for an unwanted or unexpected outcome.   Such a claim appeals to individuals' distrust of the media.   It sustains a myth.   Research using Bayesian statistics to test the difference between the real and presumed effects should be conducted.

[2]   It is a good idea to check with a librarian for various computer data bases in medicine and sport. Often these can be accessed with a personal computer, telephone modem, and printer.   The only drawback is cost.   As the connect time and number of items increases, the costs generally increase. A relatively new journal started in 1985 is Sports Search which presents the Table of Contents for various professional journals in sports psychology, sportsmedicine, and specific sports ranging from karate to swimming. It is a handy reference to keep abreast of sports.

[3]   Two causes legally acceptable for removal of a scholarship from an athlete are: (1) inadequate scholarship leading to ineligibility under school, conference, or NCAA standards; and (2) actions violating criminal or civil law, school conduct rules, departmental or team rules, thus serving as grounds for dismissal as a disciplinary problem.   Poor athletic performance is not justifiable cause in its own right. It must be seen as symptomatic of other causes such as drug use which inhibits performance and also is violation of one or more of the above conduct rules. Reasons for leveling one of these charges must be adequately documented.   The athlete must have been warned that certain behaviors were proscribed or that his or her behavior was in violation of conduct rules or threaten continued scholarship support.   Where probationary status can be granted, such action should be taken. Dismissal is to be exercises only as a last resort.

[4]   As undergraduates at Bowdoin College, we were fortunate to have been treated by Dr. Daniel Hanley, Olympic team doctor. I hope my memory does not play me false.   I recall Dr. Hanley arguing that athletes hone their kinesthetic sense and are overly sensitive to body states which are self-defined as not normal.   When

these circumstances occur, the athlete seeks medical attention. Over the years medical services and the training staff have become more elaborate. With each new service added, there is a tendency for athletes to make use of it. It may well be that, given the population served and the institutional supports that have been created, a side-effect of sports participation is a tendency toward hypochondriasis. It would be interesting to compare athletes and non-athletes during the peak ages of sport participation, and compare former athletes and non-athletes in their 30s, 40s, and 50s to see if differences exist. To fully explore the hypotheses, one also should compare participants and non-participants in their 30s, 40s, and 50s to see if the effects of continued training maintain kinesthetic awareness and a propensity toward hypochondriasis.

5   Typically three options exist: either the head coach, or the aquatics director, or the intramurals director who usually is sensitive to the demands of recreational wants of the students, faculty, and community. If administrators wish to support the swimming program, they will define the coaching position so as to include the duties of an aquatics director position. If they wish to detract from the power of the head coach, they can separate the two positions. If they wish to make the head coach's job more difficult, they can place the aquatics director under the aegis of the intramurals director. In this case, pool time for competitive swimming gets short-changed.

6   An individual can build a reputation based on strengths and weaknesses. Areas often evaluated include understanding of stroke and turn mechanics; the ability to write workouts for various strokes and distances during each phase of the season; the ability to motivate athletes; organizational acumen; the ability to use people to their best advantage; the ability to recruit; and, the ability to raise monies. No coach will be strong in all areas, although as experiences increases an understanding of the basic issues in each of these areas is developed.

7   In the long run the procedure may also reduce donations to the athletic department. Fewer donors and the consequent reduced budget may lead both athletes and department officials to seek alternative sources of funding. One source of big-dollar amounts is the commercial sector. Unfortunately, as dollar amounts get larger there is increased pressure to want some

service or product in return for expenditure. An unanticipated pressure toward increased commercialism has been stimulated. Ironically, commercialism is one aspect of athletes that many of the NCAA rule changes are intended to eliminate.

"Hey Tom, I hear that you are coaching swimming. What are you doing, giving up teaching?"
"No, I have a split appointment."
"How do you find the time for everything?"
"I get up earlier in the morning, work later at night, and have a research assistant."
"Does it interfere with research and writing?"
"No, but it shoots the weekends and cuts down on vacations."

"What does your family think of your coaching?"
"Nobody likes to hear the alarm go off early in the morning. I sometimes think the kids don't know me anymore. Last night when I came home around 11 o'clock, the dog growled at me."

"Say Tom, if you had to choose between coaching and teaching, which would you pick?"
"I really don't know."

* * * * * * * * * *

Sometimes when an individual occupies a particular role in an organization there are different social expectations held by others of what he or she should do. A situation in which there are incongruent social demands is called role conflict. There are four possible types of conflict.

First is intersender conflict -- individual A, who occupies the role, and individual B do not share similar expectations about what individual A should do. For instance, teachers of academic courses or physical education instructors who are required by school principals or departmental chairpersons to coach often express the sentiment that they are overburdened or overworked. They claim they would rather just teach.

Second is intrasender conflict -- individual A receives mixed messages from individual B about what should be done in a given role. For example, if a chairperson of a physical education department requires a coach to take responsibility for another sport besides swimming, but fails to assign priorities as to which is more important, the role conflict may follow.

Third is person-role conflict -- expectations of the role violate the personal beliefs or values of the job holder. For instance, a coach fearful of losing the job may pressure athletes to take shortcuts in studying or try to get professors to change grades to maintain eligibility. If such actions violate a personal belief that students should strive for academic excellence, and not merely survive, then person-role conflict may result.

Fourth is inter-role conflict--individual A occupies two or more roles in the same organization or in different social relationships, thus the demands of these different roles create competing cross-pressures with which the individual must cope. For instance, when a man acts as father/teacher/coach, or a woman acts as mother/professor/coach, then the various pressures of childrearing, lecturing and grading exams, as well as counseling numerous swimmers with personal problems may require a lot of juggling in one's daily schedule (Decker 1986).

Instead of role conflict another possibility exists. Sometimes an individual faces multiple pressures simply in trying to comply with the multiple expectations attached to a role. This condition is called role strain. For instance, a coach may face simultaneous demands from others--such as the faculty, administration, students, or athletes--to perform various aspects of the job better.

The coach who is also a high school teacher of academic courses, or is a physical education instructor, or is a college professor may experience various types of role conflict or strain. Generally, persons who have entered coaching at the request or demand of others (structural motive) rather than because they wanted to (personal motive) experience high levels of role conflict. Individuals who coach because they have volunteered generally express low levels of role conflict.

Similarly, coaches who prefer a single role of academic teacher, physical education instructor, or coach of a single sport both occupy a split appointment experience higher role conflict than individuals who voluntarily have sought out a split appointment.

In secondary schools, female teacher/coaches show higher levels of role conflict than the male teacher/coaches (Gehrke 1982). In college, there are no clear-cut differences between female and male teacher/coaches (Massengale and Locke 1976). It is not clear why inter-role conflict is more noticeable for females in high school than in college. Perhaps teaching and coaching activities tend to take more time in high school than in college since the high school day is more fully scheduled than in college. If teaching and coaching in high school were more time demanding, then married females would traditionally experience greater pressure to resolve inter-role conflict between family and school in favor of the family. Such a resolution typically would mean dropping out of coaching. Individuals who are college physical education instructors and coaches, or those who are professor and coach in college perhaps probably have sufficient past experience in such a dual role to know how to cope with potential role strains and conflicts.

Although some research is available on sources and correlates of role conflict among high school and college coaches, the strategies of coping usually are not discussed in any detail. Thus, the role conflicts and strains at home and at work as experienced by the professor/coach are examined.

Dealing with the family

The position of coach, like any other job, generates role conflict. As coach there are multiple obligations that have to be fulfilled. One's roles of coach and of spouse/parent generate conflict. Perhaps the major conflict involves different time schedules. Coaches for the better part of the year have to get up early (4:30 - 5:00 AM) to arrive at morning workouts on time. When the alarm goes off and the coach stumbles out of bed, the partner's sleep is disturbed. If the spouse does not need to get up, a pattern of disturbed sleep leads to fatigue, and perhaps resentment. At the other end of the day, the coach usually retires exceptionally early. Often the spouse stays up alone. This pattern also may persist on weekends. Again, resentment may surface.

Early departures and late arrivals following evening and morning practices or late night recruitment telephone calls or visits also play havoc with meal schedules. Since meal time is often the only occasion for parents and children to interact, especially in families with school-aged children or where both spouses work, the coach's absence often leaves much of the parenting to the other spouse. On those occasions when the family is together and children seek advice from the coach/parent, sometimes the coach is tempted to react to the child as just another member of the squad. Strategies learned in dealing with the athlete to maintain control, to manipulate, or effect emotional distance may get repeated when dealing with the child. The lessons learned when reacting to the manipulative strategies of athletes may heighten the coach's awareness of the child's attempted ploys. After a time, a certain degree of callousness or cynicism may develop; ploys are ignored or dismissed in a cavalier fashion. When the child tries a ploy and is ignored, the relationship between coach/parent and child becomes strained.

Taking care of the mundane tasks of shopping, going to the dry cleaners, getting the car fixed, and so forth often are complicated if the family has limited means of transportation. Getting to and from early morning practices and late afternoon or evening sessions sometimes may place stress on other members of the family. This type of strain increases as the children reach the ages where they have more activities of their own to attend and places to go, or as the number of drivers increases but the number of cars remains fixed.

Travel for recruitment, to swim meets as an observer or for scheduled competition, and to professional meetings and clinics make further demands on the coach. To compensate for these absences the coach will often spend a lot of time with the family during the off-season. Sometimes the swings from no involvement and inattention to intense involvement and constant attention also create pressures. When one parent is away, the other must pick up more responsibilities in parenting, taking care of chores, and care-giving. When the absentee parent returns, family members need to readjust to the re-allocation of tasks as the absentee resumes the temporarily abandoned roles. Alternating periods of normal role load and role strain for the partner left at home create tensions, especially in negotiating predictable role assignments. For some partners, the ambiguity of who does what and when proves to be too much. The partnership dissolves.

Coping with the faculty

Coaches, when planning the schedule of meets, usually take the NCAA championship meets for men and women as the starting points and work backward through the conference meets to the dual meet season. Practice schedules are usually fixed by a combination of availability of facilities, vacations, and time of final examinations. Although coaches keep an eye on the college or university schedule, if conflicts arise it is left to the athlete to resolve matters with the faculty. Coaches generally treat practice hours as sacred and urge swimmers not to schedule classes that conflict. If a course is required for a major and offered on a limited basis, then a conflict may be permitted. Such decisions usually are made individually. Most coaches presume that missed practices will be made up. Athletes pursuing majors that require a great deal of laboratory or field work that conflicts with practice time often are encouraged to defer enrolling in these courses until spring quarter. During the spring quarter training time is less demanding (unless it is an Olympic year). Sometimes the coach asks the swimmers not to enroll in labs or field placement courses until after completing their eligibility. In many colleges and universities it is common for athletes and non-athletes to take five or perhaps six years before completing a degree. Some educators believe that the four-year degree is going the way of penny candy, the nickel coke, and so forth.

Within any academic community some professors are protagonists of sport; some are antagonists of sport; and some professors do not care at all about sports. The antagonists often stereotype athletes. More often than not the experiences with football and basketball players are used to build the stereotype. The stereotypical athlete is seen as a perfunctory student. They attend class when they are not on the road, or when they feel like it. The athlete relies on others for getting assignments, taking notes, and structuring responses to essay questions or term papers. The athlete depends on a tutor to pre-digest materials. The athlete lacks skills in reading and writing because they have not had the time needed for study and mastery of these skills. To compensate, they hone listening skills. They enroll in easy courses, or courses where "test files" are available. They avoid difficult instructors. The football and basketball players allegedly come from a socioeconomic background where studies are a necessary evil to be endured in order to maintain eligibility and eventually to make it to the pros.

Once a professor identifies a student as an athlete, this negative stereotype is invoked and discrimination begins, even before the individual has had an opportunity to perform for the professor. Characteristically life is made difficult for the athlete. Late papers are deemed unacceptable. No make-up exams are permitted. Absences lower class recitation grades. Pop quizzes are sprung when athletes are missing due to travel.

When good grades are achieved or analytic abilities are demonstrated by an athlete, the professor expresses pleasant surprise and "fences" or marks the individual as an exception to the rule. Fortunately, most swimmers usually come from a social class background where education is valued and they have already developed solid study habits.

Faculty also invoke gender stereotypes against female athletes. Female athletes often complain that certain instructors cast aspersions on their femininity for being a swimmer or a diver. Even after almost one hundred years of heightened consciousness for females, it is the middle-aged female or the foreign female language instructor who remains most vehemently anti-athlete.

Faculty may be involved in a particular sport and are sympathetic to fellow participants. All other sports are treated as boring and outlandish. Participants in these "lesser" activities are not taken as serious athletes. Further, athletes who seriously participate in sports other that the "preferred" one are viewed as displaying a behavior which is incomprehensible. Why would somebody do something as foolish as swim back and forth, going nowhere? Who would be crazy enough to chase a golf ball, only to put it in a hole 9, 18, or x number of times?

Where faculty are antagonistic and/or have little leverage in ensuring that sports do not conflict with the academic timetable, they tend to exercise their authority in the classroom. Coaches and athletes over the years come to recognize which of these faculty are to be avoided. New faculty and graduate assistants may prove to be troublesome until their stance and reputations become known.

The athletes also are quick not only to recognize which faculty are protagonists of sport, but also which courses are easy. Some coaches, instead of simply relying on this informal method of identifying courses, when counseling athletes refer to a detailed file of the "hard" and "easy" professors. When a swimmer is weak academically, or looking for a light quarter or semester, such coaches simply check the file and arrange a light schedule. This paternalistic practice protects the swimmer and may maintain eligibility. Conversely, such paternalism may coddle the athlete to the point that an entire curriculum is watered-down. The student may end up under-prepared and with a virtually worthless degree upon graduation.

Athletic departments and coaches have been castigated, and rightly so, for arranging easy course curricula for athletes. The fact that such a strategy can be effected leads to a broader indictment. It raises fundamental questions: How well are department heads/chairs monitoring the faculty within their departments? Are administrators sensitive to weaker faculty, departments, and programs throughout the institution? Until the opportunity for selecting the easy path has been closed, the practice of paternalistic course selection will probably continue.[1]

For coaches who hold a split appointment as professor/coach an issue that must be resolved is: What is the relative emphasis to be placed on academics and sports when advising the student-athletes? Acting as a faculty member, the individual automatically assumes that studies take precedence. The standard list of reasons are easily recited when advising student-athletes on scholastic matters. As one becomes more mature as a scholar, the professor has more to offer the student. The professor also demands more, unless some perspective is maintained on just how much material a class can master within the time frame of a quarter or semester.

While acting as a coach, it is easy to assume that athletics take precedence; after all, job security is tied to the performance of the athletes. As the coach becomes more experienced one becomes more technically proficient and incorporates more refinements into the program, thereby placing increased demands on the athletes. To reconcile these cross-pressures, the professor/coach must take the stance that while acting in either role, all one can do is act as a facilitator. The ultimate decision on how priorities are set rests with the student-athlete. Although the professor/coach can offer an opinion on how priorities are structured, especially if they are ill-conceived and may have a detrimental effect on the athlete, the mentor must recognize that it is ultimately the student-athlete who is responsible.

Professor/coach as split appointment

Administrators in institutions that have highly competitive athletic programs are reluctant to hire coaches as split appointments with responsibilities as professor/coach. There are administrative pressures to avoid split appointments. In order to hire an individual who serves as a coach and faculty member, credentials have to be approved by both the athletic department and the academic department where one will teach. Both sets of administrators and faculty, as well as athletes and students, will have to meet the candidate during the interview process. Administrative approval involves both chains of command; salary has to be okayed in two budget reviews. If the candidate has tenure as a faculty member and is hired as a coach, then a potential problem arises: What action should be taken if the individual serving as the coach gets fired? The academic department may be forced to add the individual as a fully tenured faculty member. Therefore, the academic department is reluctant to accept the individual on a tenure track since academic departments do not want to lose any degrees of freedom in tenuring faculty. Also tenured faculty with increased experience and rank become more costly to the institution. As costs increase each department strives more diligently to avoid the responsibility of paying any portion or the entire salary of the split appointment.

In institutions open to the possibility of hiring split appointments administrators make the following assumptions. First, they assume that the professor/coach is competent in both areas. Second, they assume that the individual can fulfill both types of job demands without experiencing conflict. Third, both teaching and coaching require the same communication role skills. Fourth, both teaching and coaching require technical skills with the latter usually being more applied. Fifth, they assume that the individual is equally interested in both jobs (Chu 1981 suggested points 2, 4, and 5). Chu, reporting on his own research on teacher/coaches, suggests that males holding split appointments expend approximately triple the time in coaching that they do in teaching. Females in similar positions spend almost twice the time in coaching that they do in teaching. Chu (1981: 162) argues that the roles are distinct and most people prefer coaching over teaching.

Clearly, professor/coach is a time-consuming occupation. For the coach in the more competitive program, there is greater pressure to expend more time in preparation, whether it is recruiting, reading the professional literature, or keeping up with the flow of paper work in the daily routine. The nature of the pressure also mounts as one moves from the position of volunteer coach to paid coach, and from an assistant coach to a head coach. As a volunteer one's tasks are quite limited. The head coach recognizes that other roles take precedence over coaching. Coaching responsibilities are assigned to ensure that a balance is maintained; after all, the head coach does not want to lose free help. Once the individual moves into a paid position, the job description becomes fixed. One is expected to expend the time and energy necessary to carry out assigned duties.

As an assistant coach, role demands are not quite as pressure-packed as those of a head coach. The individual moves from a position of fairly specific sets of obligations to a position with an expanded number of demands. As a head coach the responsibilities multiply even more.

The typical role cluster as a faculty member includes the responsibilities of teaching, conducting research and publication, holding student conferences, directing theses, and doing committee work. As a volunteer coach, there is time available to fulfill obligations in both teaching and coaching. As a paid assistant coach holding a split appointment, negotiations may be needed for release from certain areas of responsibility or at least reduced expectations. As a head coach, such negotiations are mandatory. Moreover faculty may view the role of "coach" differently, depending on the nature of the commitment. In the case of a volunteer coach, faculty may express the view that the individual is merely acting out one's fantasy or developing a stronger leisure time identity. In the case of a paid coach, be it assistant or head coach, the faculty may see the position as an integral part of the person's career development. The more time that is spent as a coach, the more likely that the affected faculty will express a concern over which career may eventually be chosen. It is easier to generate faculty and athletic department support for a split appointment as an assistant than as a head coach.[2]

Similarly, in athletic departments that pride themselves as being highly competitive (NCAA I and sometimes NCAA II schools) there is some reluctance to define the head coaching position as a split appointment. At the college level, in many NCAA III or NAIA schools, generally there is less emphasis on producing top-flight programs and elite performers. Historically, there has been a greater acceptance of the split appointment for the head coach.

The individual who aspires to occupational success as either professor or coach, or both must be organized and capable of handling pressure. With experience, the individual holding a split appointment becomes increasingly proficient in conducting coaching and professorial roles. Most situations that earlier involved any role conflict have been resolved or accommodations negotiated.

Interestingly, faculty view the roles of volunteer, assistant, and head coach differently in the commitment required and prestige granted. If a professor is serving as a volunteer coach, other faculty tend to see the commitment as "low key." The role is viewed as providing a break from the pressures of work. It is part of the leisure-time identity of an individual. The volunteer position is seen as a form of service to the university or college community, noteworthy as an altruistic action, but little else.

An assistant coach, if receiving remuneration--pay, release time, or equipment--is taken more seriously by faculty colleagues. The commitment of time is greater and the background and training of the individual presumably is better than that of the volunteer. In regions of the United States and in schools where sports are highly valued, the assistant coach accrues a modicum of prestige. But in regions where sports are seen as "play breaks" from work or leisure time activities, coaching is a low prestige occupation. The designation of "coach" may be bandied about in conversations or in greetings, but usually is done so in a tongue-in-cheek manner.

When an individual occupies the position of head coach, then the individual is viewed by academic colleagues as holding two full-time jobs. The individual takes on the identity of coach and all the trappings of office. The level of prestige attached to the position in part flows from how competitive the program is and its reputation. The smaller the program's size, the lower its reputation, and the less competitive, generally the less prestige is attached to the coaching position. Conversely, as these factors increase, so does the prestige accrued. Unless a coach is involved in a highly competitive program, one is perceived as having a great deal of free time. But one who coaches and has some other job is seen as fully employed. If both jobs are viewed as time consuming, then the individual is seen by friends as over-committed and "different."

A misperception among friends and colleagues that sometimes follows one's entry into coaching is that the coach automatically becomes knowledgeable on how to cope with a variety of sports-based injuries. Friends may ask for diagnoses and suggested therapies. The coach must always preface any replies with the standard admonition that the individual should check with a doctor.

Strategies for coping as a split appointment

Individuals may follow a number of strategies for reducing role strain or role conflict (Massengale 1981). Four are identified in this section.

Neutralization.-One way to reduce role strain is to deny the veracity of claims made by others. Coaches in dealing with the array of others--ranging from administrators to fans--often feel that everybody always wants something. To cope with the pressures brought about by demands for changes in behavior, the coach may simply dismiss the request. The dismissal may be prefaced with a remark which undercuts the authority of the other to make moral demands of the coach. For instance, an administrator may request that a coach cease an extra-legal action, some practice that is on the fringes of illegality, but not clearly defined as illegal according to NCAA rules and interpretations. The action in the coach's eyes is one taken by all coaches. Not to follow the practice would place one at a disadvantage. In this circumstance, the coach "blows off" the request claiming: "Why should I do what he says? That person has never coached and doesn't know the problems we face."

A related tactic to ease conflicting demands is to trivialize them. The coach reduces the importance attached to expectations of others. "They don't pay me enough to put up with this amount of grief." The coach reassigns priorities to expected tasks. The coach may argue that: "Others are asking too much of me." In effect, the coach neutralizes the demands of others. The tasks really are not necessary for the satisfactory performance of the jobs. By reducing, dismissing, or eliminating the tasks normally required, the professor/coach reduces the number of cross-pressures to a manageable level.

Massengale (1981) suggests that the strategy for reducing conflict through redefinition and reorganization may also be accomplished at the

145

institutional level. One way to reduce pressure is to change the coach's interpretation of the expectations and the rewards of the job. As long as the job receives low pay, has long hours, lacks security, and lacks credentials then coaches will tend to protect their turf by reducing the pressures exerted by others and to maintain their self-esteem by devaluing the moral claims of others. To alter this perception, the public and the audiences served by the coach must be educated to upgrade the status of the coach. The educational system must improve the reward structure for the job and provide greater job security.

Role switch.-Another strategy for reducing role conflict is to withdraw from the obligations, demands, and duties assigned to one role and embrace those attached to the other. For instance, if the individual holds a coach/professor appointment and finds the demands of academe to be onerous, then the tendency is to reassign one's priorities by defining coaching duties as primary and professorial duties as secondary. This permits withdrawal from committee work, escape from the pressures of publish or perish, and lets one pursue a life style that one may view as more acceptable.

"Super coach."-Another strategy for handling role strain or conflict is for the individual to accommodate to the demands (Massengale [1981] calls this strategy adaptation and compromise.) The split appointee accepts the contradictory pressures or heightened demands, treats them as a challenge, and becomes extremely organized and efficient. One becomes "super coach/super prof" like "super mom." The individual buys a computer to speed scanning of files and records. The coach looks for time-saving ways to handle the daily routine--such as buying an answering machine for both office phone and home; returning calls that accumulate during the day at one time; and handling correspondence by dictation. The individual always solicits assistance for more support personnel in each office (the athletic department and the faculty department). The individual learns how to delegate. The individual with a split appointment tends to mix autocratic and consultative styles of decision-making by placing a lot of emphasis on acquiring the maximum amount of information available in the shortest possible time.

Drop out.-Finally, if all else fails, the individual can drop out of each position and find a new job. If the individual withdraws, no one will be surprised since coaching has a fairly high attrition given the long hours and low pay.

When an individual leaves sports or coaching, a variety of different perspectives are used to account for the move. Earlier accounts portray withdrawal from coaching as a form of "social death" fraught with all the same adjustments that any retiree faces: loss of friends and acquaintances; the severing of ties with professional associations; loss of prestige or reduced self esteem; reduction in salary; and removal from public view. These accounts tend to dwell on the negative aspects of exiting from a job or retiring. More recent accounts simply treat leaving coaching as a status transformation, moving form one social position and its roles to another (Blinde and Greendorfer 1985; Greendorfer and Blinde 1985).

Explanations for withdrawal from coaching tend to fall into two camps. First are the sociological studies that emphasize shifts in personal relationships which affect the structural and personal motives for coaching. Weiss and Sisley (1984) investigated reasons for dropping out as a coach in youth basketball programs. Structural motives offered by former coaches to account for their withdrawal include: (1) role conflict--wanted to spend more time with the family, conflicts with the regular job, too time consuming, or other leisure activities are more interesting; (2) role shift in parenting--the son/daughter no longer is involved in the sport or program; (3) role strain--too many problems in dealing with unqualified officials, a lack of support from program personnel, disagreement with the program philosophy; (4) personal motives--no longer enjoying positive feelings like one used to when first coached.

Second are psychological studies in which college coaches claim a need to withdraw due to feelings of burnout. Caccesse and Mayerberg (1984) surveyed NCAA and AIAW coaches at division I and found that female head coaches more often expressed feelings of burnout than male coaches. Female dropouts tended to be slightly younger than males, and have fewer years of experience than males. Research also suggested that for those who remain in the coaching profession for a number of years, job satisfaction is good, and that those who feel stress due to role conflict, role strain, or shifts in attitudes tend to voluntarily withdraw.

Unfortunately, no studies appear to exist that provide statistics on the numbers of coaches fired in specific sports, or those who withdraw because they no longer can put up with the increased pressures in colleges and universities generated by expanding bureaucracy and greater emphasis on accountability. Similarly, research is needed to ascertain whether former coaches are better off financially as active or retired. One suspects that job turnover is probably not as high among intercollegiate head coaches in swimming as in football or basketball. Most of the turnover probably occurs among volunteers and assistant coaches. To verify these suspicions data are needed.

Summary

--Coaches belong to many organizations. They occupy roles that may exert cross-pressures on them with various duties to be performed. Such role conflict occurs as coach and spouse/parent. It also occurs as coach/professor. The magnitude of these conflicts depends on the demands created while individuals serve as volunteer, assistant, or head coach. As responsibilities increase in either role, or both, the cross-pressures on time and energy mount.

--Resolution of role conflict may lead the individual to "opt out" of one role in favor or another. It also may lead to a role shift. An alternative strategy is to become super-organized in order to adapt and accommodate to the pressure of both roles. Finally, one can withdraw from coaching and seek a new profession.

REVIEW QUESTIONS

1. What are the four types of role conflict? What is role strain?

2. In Chapter 8 role conflict is discussed for the parent/coach assuming that the individual is married. The focus was on interaction between spouses. Assume that the coach is a single parent and describe what kinds of conflicts might be found.

3. In Chapter 8 the split appointment of professor/coach is examined. Many people who coach, especially in high school, YMCAs, and U.S. Swimming programs, carry two jobs. Identify what kinds of role conflicts these people might have.

4. Which of the strategies for coping with role strain would you choose or have you chosen?

NOTES

1   From the coach's and athlete's perspectives, if the athlete wishes to place a higher priority on sports than on academics, then at least for the short-term, the academic path of least resistance is most rational. Conversely, if the athlete wishes to place a higher priority on academics, such a strategy obviously would not be followed.

2   As the emphasis on academic excellence increases, so do the public utterances of the litany that teaching is a full time "calling." A lesser commitment may be seen by some faculty as heretical.

In part, this is a case study of the college swimming coach that looks at the social issues and roles that make up the social worlds in which the coach must act from day-to-day. It is also a primer for the student who anticipates becoming a swimming coach or the new assistant coach just beginning to serve an apprenticeship. For the student in physical education it provides an introduction to a body of literature not normally read. Similarly, for the student in the behavioral sciences, it taps a literature in swimming and physical education usually overlooked. Some basic sociological concepts drawn from the traditional literature on role analysis are utilized as are some basic principles from social psychology to look at the careers of coaches as they move from apprentices, to assistant coaches, and finally to head coaches. Practical lessons are based on experience are included to ensure that the reader gains both a theoretical and practical understanding about the career of collegiate swimming coach.

The apprenticeship role of the assistant coach is covered in some detail looking at the variety of administrative, supervisory, and on-deck responsibilities that must mastered. How head coaches build a staff of assistant coaches, and the advantages and disadvantages of working with volunteer or paid assistants are reviewed.

Questions that head coaches must ask when looking for jobs are suggested. How does one network? How does one read job advertisements? What are the job markers to which to one must be sensitive? What issues should be examined when evaluating a possible job opening? More specifically, what are the questions the job candidate must ask of the AD about the school, the program, and the community? Social issues that coaches must address as they administer a swimming program within an academic environment are discussed. The organizational tasks and communication skills that must be mastered for a coach to administer a program effectively are outlined in some detail. Similarly, attention is paid to the different styles of leadership that coaches may elect to use and the various philosophies of management that coaches may follow in running a program.

The roles that college and university swimming coaches play as they interact with a variety of people both inside of the academic and sporting communities--such as the athletic director(AD), the sports information director(SID), the physician, the trainer, the aquatics director, the academic advisor, secretaries, janitors, food and housing services personnel, and campus security personnel--and outside of the academic and community--such as representatives from the conference, NCAA, and ASCA offices and parents are discussed. Finally, some of the role strains and conflicts that coaches face who hold a split appointment as a coach/faculty member are identified and some of the strategies used to ameliorate or solve these problems are presented.

Hopefully, this book highlights the importance of mastering the social skills and social psychological principles needed to coach student-athletes and to administer a program as well as the traditional incorporation of scientific principles of the sport.

The focus is exclusively on the college and university swimming coach. However, the reader should not lose sight of the fact that there are many other mentors in the sport--such as swimming instructors teaching infants, toddlers, children and adults beginning swimming; age-group coaches working with swimmers to achieve various competitive time standards in each age bracket; YMCA coaches working with summer league and national teams; and interscholastic coaches working/teaching in the high schools and prep schools. Each contributes to the strength of the swimming in the United States. Although in some ways the careers and experiences of non-college coaches differ from those of college coaches, the world of swimming shares enough similarities so that many of the lessons learned by examining the experiences of the collegiate college are transferable and may be of benefit to any of the other coaches.

REFERENCES

The American Swimming Coaches Association.
   c1985   Certification....an explanation for
                coaches. the finals.

The American Swimming Coaches Association (ASCA).
   1986   "An interview with Laurie Lawrence:
                Australian ASCA Coach of the Year 1985."
                ASCA Newsletter (May/June): 15-21.

The American Swimming Coaches Association.
   c1986   ASCA The Certified Swimming Coach: A
                Guide for Employers. the finals.

Anderson, W.G. and Barrette, G.T.
   1978   "Teacher behavior." in W.G. Anderson and
                G.T.Barrette (Eds.) What's Going on in
                Gym: Descriptive Studies of Physical
                Education Classes. Monograph 1. Motor
                Skills: Theory into Practice.

Anselmi, Kurt.
   1986   "Certification update:" ASCA Newsletter
                (May/June): 25.

Armistead, David.
   1980   "Coaching as management." in Robert M.
                Ousley (Ed.) World Clinic Year Book.
                American Swimming Coaches Association.
                Fort Lauderdale, FL. 1980. pp. 29-90.

Bain, L.
   1978   "Differences in values implicit in
                teaching and coaching behaviors."
                Research Quarterly 49, 1: 5-11.

Bales, Robert F.
   1966   "Task roles and social roles in problem-
                solving groups." in B.J. Biddle and E.J.
                Thomas (Eds.) Role Theory: Concepts and
                Research. John Wiley and Sons, NY. pp.
                254-263.

Ball, Donald W.
   1976   "Failure in sport." American
                Sociological Review 41 (August): 726-
                739.

Becker, Howard S.
    1972   "A school is a lousy place to learn
                anything in." in Blanche Geer (Ed.)
                Learning to Work. Sage. Beverly Hills,
                CA. pp. 89-109.

Betz, Michael.
    1981   "From whence accountability?" Nursing
                and Health Care 11, 1 (November): 482-
                484, 486 & 506.

Blinde, Elaine M. and Greendorfer, Susan L.
    1985   "A reconceptualization of the process of
                leaving the role of competitive
                athlete." International Review of
                Sociology of Sport 20/1+2: 87-93.

Boesch, John.
    1977   "A professional look at promoting our
                sport." in Robert M. Ousley (Ed.) World
                Clinic Year Book. American Swimming
                Coaches Association. Fort Lauderdale,
                FL. pp. 19-31.

Broderick, Robert.
    1984   "Non-certified coaches." JOPERD 53 (May-
                June): 38-39, & 53.

Brown, Barbara.
    1985   "Factors influencing the process of
                withdrawal by female adolescents from
                the role of competitive age-group
                swimmer." Sociology of Sport Journal 2:
                111-129.

Bussard, Ray.
    1972   "Tennessee swimming: The winning edge."
                Swimming Technique. Reprinted in Robert
                M. Ousley (Ed.) World Clinic Year Book.
                American Swimming Coaches Association.
                Fort Lauderdale, FL. 1969-1973. pp. 25-
                26.

Caccese, Thomas M. and Mayerberg, Cathleen K.
    1984   "Gender differences in perceived burnout
                of college coaches." Journal of Sport
                Psychology 6: 279-288.

Carron, Albert V.
1978   "Role behavior and the coach-athlete
            interaction." International Review of
            Sport Sociology 13, 2: 51-65.

Carron, Albert V.
1980   Social Psychology of Sport. Mouvement
            Publications, Ithaca, NY.

Carron, Albert V. and Bennett, Bonnie B.
1977   "Compatibility in the coach-athlete
            dyad." Research Quarterly 48 (December):
            671-679.

Cheffers, J.T.F. and Mancini, Victor H.
1978   "Teacher-student interaction." in W.G.
            Anderson and G.T. Barrette (Eds.) What's
            Going on in Gym: Descriptive Studies of
            Physical Education classes. Monograph 1.
            Motor Skills: Theory into Practice.

Chelladurai, P.
1984   "Discrepancy between preferences and
            perceptions of leadership behavior and
            satisfaction of athletes in varying
            sports." Journal of Sport Psychology 6:
            27-41.

Chelladurai, P. and Arnott, M.
1985   "Decision styles in coaching:
            Preferences of basketball players."
            Research Quarterly for Exercise and
            Sport 56, 1: 15-24.

Chelladurai, P. and Carron, Albert V.
1983   "Athletic maturity and preferred
            leadership."   Journal of Sport
            Psychology 5: 371-380.

Chelladurai, P. and Haggerty, T.R.
1978   "A normative model for decision styles
            in coaching." Athletic Administrator 13:
            6-9.

Chelladurai, P. and Saleh, S.D.
1978   "Preferred leadership in sport."
            Canadian Journal of Applied Sport
            Sciences 3: 85-97.

Chu, Donald.
    1981   "Origins of teacher/coach role conflict:
                A reaction to Massengale's paper." in
                S.L. Greendorfer and A. Yiannakis (Eds.)
                Sociology of Sport: Diverse
                Perspectives. Leisure Press. West Point,
                NY. pp. 158-163.

Coakley, Jay J.
    1986   Sport in Society: Issues and
                Controversies. Times Mirror/Mosby
                College Publishing. St. Louis, MO.

Counsilman, James E.
    1977   Competitive Swimming Manual for Coaches
                and Swimmers. Counsilman Co. Inc.
                Bloomington, IN. 1977.

Cratty, Bryant J.
    1983   Psychology in Contemporary Sport:
                Guidelines for Coaches and Athletes.
                Second Edition. Prentice-Hall. Englewood
                Cliffs, NJ. 1983. Chapter 10. "The
                Coach." pp. 213-248.

Daland, Peter.
    1975   "What it takes to be a successful
                swimming coach." in Robert M. Ousley
                (Ed.) World Clinic Year Book. American
                Swimming Coaches Association. Fort
                Lauderdale, FL. pp. 45-54.

Daniels, C.M.
    1906   "How American swimming was
                revolutionized." The Illustrated Outdoor
                News 6 (31 March): 2.

Danielson, R.R., Zelhart, P.F., Drake, C.J.
    1975   "Multidimensional scaling and factor
                analysis of coaching behavior as
                perceived by high school hockey
                players." Research Quarterly 46: 323-
                334.

de B. Handley, L.
    1906   "The outdoor swimming season of 1906."
                The Illustrated Outdoor News (November):
                132-133.

Decker, June I.
    1986   "Role conflict of teachers/coaches in
                small colleges." Sociology of Sport
                Journal 3: 356-365.

Dummer, Gail, Rosen, Lionel W., Heusner, William W.,
and Roberts, Pamela J.
    1986   "Weight modification behaviors of age-
                group competitive swimmers." A Paper
                Presented at The World Clinic Program,
                ASCA World Clinic '86, Dallas, TX,
                September 12.

Edwards, Harry H.
    1973   Sociology of Sport. Dorsey. Homewood,
                IL.

Fiedler, Decky and Beach, Lee Roy.
    1982   "The sport choice--A decision/expectancy
                model." Journal of Sport Psychology 4:
                81-91.

Fisher, Craig A., Mancini, Victor H., Hirsch, Ronald
L., Proulx, Thomas J., and Staurowsky, Ellen J.
    1982   "Coach-athlete interactions and team
                climate." Journal of Sport Psychology 4:
                388-404.

Fleishman, E.A.
    1957a   The Leadership Opinion Questionnaire. in
                L.M. Stodgill and A.E. Coons (Eds.)
                Leader Behavior: Its Description and
                Measurement. The Ohio State University,
                Columbus, OH. pp. 120-133.

Fleishman, E.A.
    1957b   "A leader behavior description for
                industry." in L.M. Stodgill and A.E.
                Coons (Eds.) Leader Behavior: Its
                Description and Measurement. The Ohio
                State University, Columbus, OH.

Freas, Sam.
    1980   "The promotion of swimming." in Robert
                M. Ousley (Ed.) World Clinic Year Book.
                American Swimming Coaches Association.
                Fort Lauderdale, FL. pp. 147-156.

Friedman, Lawrence and Percival, Robert V.
1981   The Roots of Justice: Crime and
          Punishment in Alameda County,
          California, 1870-1910. University of
          North Carolina, Chapel Hill.

Gambril, Don.
1983   "Effective use of assistant coaches." in
          Robert M. Ousley (Ed.) World Clinic Year
          Book. American Swimming Coaches
          Association. Fort Lauderdale, FL. pp.
          169-176.

Gambril, Don and Bay, Alfred.
1984   Swimmer and Team. Alfred Bay. Palo Alto,
          CA.

Gehrke, N.J.
1982   "Teacher's role conflicts; a grounded
          theory in process." Journal of Teacher
          Education 33: 41-46.

Glaser, Nathan and Strauss, Anselm.
1971   Status Passage. Aldine-Atherton.
          Chicago, IL.

Goffman, Erving.
1959   The Presentation of Self in Everyday
          Life. Doubleday Anchor. Garden City, NY.

Goffman, Erving.
1967   Interaction Ritual: Essays on Face-to-
          Face Behavior. Doubleday Anchor. Garden
          City, NY.

Gould, Daniel and Martens, Rainer.
1979   "Attitudes of volunteer coaches toward
          significant youth sport issues."
          Research Quarterly 50, 3: 369-380.

Gould, Daniel, Feltz, Deborah, Horn, Thelma S., Weiss,
Maureen R., and Mugno, Denise A.
1982   "Reasons for attrition in competitive
          swimming." Journal of Sport Behavior 5,
          3 (September): 155-165.

Greendorfer, Susan L. and Blinde, Elaine M.
1985   "'Retirement' from intercollegiate
          sports: Theoretical and empirical
          considerations." Sociology of Sport
          Journal 2: 101-110.

Halpin, A.W. and Winer, B.J.
1957   "A factorial study of the leader
            behavior description." in L.M. Stodgill
            and A.E. Coons (Eds.) Leader Behavior:
            Its Description and Measurement. The
            Ohio State University.

Hannula, Dick.
1984   "Hannula's hints: Taper." The Finals
            Newsletter (Fall/Winter).

Hart, Barbara A., Hasbrook, Cynthia A., and Mathes,
Sharon A.
1986   "An examination of the reduction in the
            number of female interscholastic
            coaches." Research Quarterly for
            Exercise and Sport 57, 1: 68-77.

Hastings, Donald W.
1983   "The ethos of Masters swimming."
            International Review of Sport Sociology
            3, 18: 31-50.

Hastings, Donald W. and Provol, George E.
1972   "Pharmacists attitudes toward
            contraceptives." Journal of American
            Pharmaceutical Association NS 12 No. 2
            (February): 74-75 & 81.

Hastings, Donald W. and Wantland, Suzanne.
1986   Guidelines for Preparing for the SEC
            Women's Swimming and Diving
            Championships. University of Tennessee,
            Knoxville, March 15. (manuscript report)

Hendry, L.B.
1968   "Assessment of personality traits in the
            coach-swimmer relationship, and a
            preliminary examination of the father-
            figure stereotype." Research Quarterly
            39, 3: 543-551.

Hendry, L.B.
1969   "A personality study of highly
            successful and 'ideal' swimming
            coaches." Research Quarterly 40, 2
            (May): 299-304.

Hendry, L.B.
    1972   "The coaching stereotype." in H.T.A.
                Whiting (Ed.) Readings in Sport
                Psychology. Henry Kimpton. London.

Holmen, Milton G. and Parkhouse, Bonnie L.
    1981   "Trends in the selection of coaches for
                female athletes: A demographic inquiry."
                Research Quarterly for Exercise and
                Sport 52, 1: 9-18.

Horn, Thelma S.
    1983   "The Michigan swim study: what motivates
                competitive youth swimmers?" Swimming
                World and Junior Swimmer 24, 3 (March):
                21-22.

Horne, Tammy and Carron, Albert V.
    1985   "Compatibility of coach-athlete
                relationships." Journal of Sport
                Psychology 7: 137-149.

Hughes, Everett C.
    1951   "Studying the nurse's work." American
                Journal of Nursing 51 (May): 294-295.

Ingham, Alan G.
    1975   "Occupational subcultures in the work
                world of sport." in Donald W. Ball and
                John W. Loy (Eds.) Sport and the Social
                Order. Contributions to the Sociology of
                Sport. Addison-Wesley, MA. pp. 395-455.

Ingram, Doug.
    1981   "Business aspects of coaching." in
                Robert M. Ousley (Ed.) World Clinic Year
                Book. American Swimming Coaches
                Association. Fort Lauderdale, FL. pp.
                15-40.

Kelly, John R.
    1983   Leisure Identities and Interactions.
                George Allen and Unwin. London.

Korten, D.C.
    1962   "Situational determinants of leadership
                structure. Journal of Conflict
                Resolution 6: 222-235.

Lanning, Wayne.
1979   "Coach and athlete personality
            interaction: A critical variable in
            athletic success." Journal of Sport
            Psychology 1: 262-267.

Lapchick, Richard E.
1986   "Sports and apartheid: The world closes
            in." in Richard E. Lapchick (Ed.)
            Fractured Focus: Sport as a Reflection
            of Society. Lexington Books-D.C. Heath.
            Lexington, MA. pp. 369-376.

Leonard, John.
1980   "The assistant coach: Choosing and
            training the right person." Swimmers
            Coach 2, 1 (January/February): 6-8.

Libby, B.
1982   "What keeps coaches going?"   National
            Forum 62, 1: 17-18.

Locke, Lawrence F. and Massengale, John D.
1978   "Role conflict in teacher/coaches."
            Research Quarterly 49, 2 (May): 162-
            174.

Lopiano, Donna A.
1986   "The certified coach: a central figure."
            JOPERD 57 (March): 34-38.

Loy, John W.
1968   "Sociopyschological attributes
            associated with early adoption of a
            sport innovation." The Journal of
            Psychology 70: 141-147.

Loy, John W., McPherson, Barry D., and Kenyon, Gerald.
1978   Sport and Social Systems: A Guide to the
            Analysis of Problems and Literature.
            Addison-Wesley. Reading, MA.

Loy, John L. and Sage, George H.
1978   "Athletic personnel in the academic
            market place: A study of the
            interorganizational mobility patterns of
            college coaches." Sociology of Work and
            Occupations 5, 4: 446-469.

Lott, A.J. and Lott, B.E.
1965   "Group cohesiveness as interpersonal
            attraction: A review of relationships
            with antecedent and consequent
            variables." Psychological Bulletin 64:
            259-302.

Maglischo, Ernest W.
1982   Swimming Faster: A Comprehensive Guide
            to the Science of Swimming. Mayfield.
            Palo Alto, CA.

Martin, Garry and Hrycaiko, Dennis.
1983   "Effective behavioral coaching: What's
            it all about?" Journal of Sport
            Psychology 5: 8-20.

Massengale, John D.
1974   "Coaching as an occupational
            subculture." Phi Delta Kappan 56
            (October): 140-142.

Massengale, John D.
1981   "Role/conflict and the teacher/coach:
            Some occupation causes and
            considerations for the sport
            sociologist" in S.L. Greendorfer and A.
            Yiannakis (Eds.) Sociology of Sport:
            Diverse Perspectives. Leisure Press.
            West Point, NY. pp. 149-157.

Massengale, John D. and Locke, Lawrence F.
1976   "Perceived and experienced role conflict
            among teacher/coaches." in National
            College Physical Education for Men.
            University of Illinois at Chicago
            Circle: Chicago. pp. 121-124.

McCall, George J. and Simmons, J.L.
1978   Identities and Interactions. Free Press.
            NY.

McElroy, Mary A.
1981   "A comparison of sport and nonsport
            occupational aspirations among
            disadvantaged youth." Journal of Sport
            Psychology 3: 58-68.

McPherson, Barry D., Marteniuk, R., Tihanyi, J., and
Clark, W.
1980   "The social system of age group
            swimming: The perception of swimmers,
            parents, and coaches." Canadian Journal
            of Applied Sports Science 5, 3: 142-
            145.

McPherson, Barry D., Marteniuk, R., Tihanyi, J., and
Clark, W.
1980   "Age group swimming: Review of
            literature." Canadian Journal of Applied
            Sports Science 5, 3: 110-131.

McPherson, Barry D.
1981   "Socialization into and through sport
            involvement." in Gunther R.F. Luschen
            and George H. Sage (Eds.) Handbook of
            Social Science of Sport. Stipes Pub. Co.
            Champaign, IL. pp. 246-273.

Mechikoff, Robert A. and Kozar, Bill (Eds.)
1983   Sport Psychology: The Coach's
            Perspective. Charles C. Thomas.
            Springfield, IL.

Meyer, Judy.
1982   "Masters swimming in the total program."
            in Robert M. Ousley (Ed.) World Clinic
            Year Book. American Swimming Coaches
            Association. Fort Lauderdale, FL. pp.
            271-280.

Mihovilovic, Miro A.
1968   "The status of former sportsmen."
            International Review of Sport Sociology
            3: 73-96.

Miller, Bob.
1977   "Tapering: what's it all about?"
            Swimming World and Junior Swimmer 18, 8
            (August): 6.

Monaghan, Peter.
1985   "Athletes' academic advisers ask
            colleges for increased authority and job
            security." The Chronicle of Higher
            Education XXXI No. 14 (December 4): 37 &
            39.

163

Mugno, Denise A.
    1983   "The Michigan swim study: why are young
                swimmers dropping out?" <u>Swimming World
                and Junior Swimmer</u> 24, 4 (April): 27,
                29-30.

Officer, Sara A. and Rosenfeld, Lawrence B.
    1985   "Self-disclosure to male and female
                coaches by female high school athletes."
                <u>Journal of Sport Psychology</u> 7: 360-370.

Ogilvie, Bruce C.
    1979   "The sport psychologist and his
                professional identity." in Peter Klavora
                and Juri V. Daniel (Eds.) <u>Coach,
                Athlete, and the Sport Psychologist</u>.
                University of Toronto, Ontario. pp. 43-
                55.

Pettigrew, J. Bell.
    1888   <u>Animal Locomotion or Walking, Swimming,
                and Flying with a Dissertation on
                Aeronautics</u>. Appleton. NY.

Purdy, Dean A., Haufler, Steven E., and Eitzen, D.
Stanley.
    1981   "Stress among child athletes:
                perceptions by parents, coaches, and
                athletes." <u>Journal of Sport Behavior</u> 4,
                1: 33-46.

Reese, Randy.
    c1985   <u>Building a Championship Season with
                Randy Reese</u>. T. & G. Enterprises.
                Northport, AL.

Rog, James A.
    1984   "Teaching and coaching: The ultimate
                challenge." <u>JOPERD</u> 55 (August): 48-49.

Roundy, Elmo and Roh, Les.
    1973   "Recruiting: What influences the
                prospects." <u>Scholastic Coach</u>: 14-15.

Roy, James A.
    1984   "Teaching and coaching: the ultimate
                challenge." <u>JOPERD</u> 55 (August): 48-49.

Rushall, Brent S.
1979   "Coaches and sport psychology."
            International Journal of Sport
            Psychology 10, 3: 164-167.

Rushall, Brent S. and Jamieson, John.
1979   "The prediction of swimming performance
            from behavioral information: A further
            note." Canadian Journal of Applied
            Sports Science 4, 2: 158-159.

Rushall, Brent S. and Leet, Donald.
1979   "The prediction of swimming performance
            in competition from behavioral
            information." Canadian Journal of
            Applied Sports Science 4, 2: 154-157.

Rushall, Brent S. and Pettinger, John.
1969   "An evaluation of the effect of various
            reinforcers used as motivators in
            swimming." Research Quarterly 40, 3
            (October): 540-545.

Rushall, Brent S. and Smith, Kenneth C.
1979   "The modification of the quality and
            quantity of behavior categories in a
            swimming coach." Journal of Sport
            Psychology 1: 138-150.

Sabock, Ralph.
1973   The Coach. W.B. Saunders. Philadelphia.
            PA.

Sage, George H.
1974   "Machiavellianism among college and high
            school coaches." in George H. Sage (Ed.)
            Sport and American Society. Addison-
            Wesley. Reading, MA.

Sage, George H.
1975   "Socialization of coaches: Antecedents
            to coaches beliefs and behaviors."
            Proceedings of the National College
            Physical Education Association for Men.
            pp. 124-132.

Sage, George H.
    1975   "An occupational analysis of the college
                coach." in Donald W. Ball and John W.
                Loy (Eds.) Sport and the Social Order.
                Contributions to the Sociology of Sport.
                Addison-Wesley. Reading, MA. pp. 395-
                455.

Sage, George H.
    1980   "Sociology of physical educator/coaches:
                The personal attributes controversy."
                Research Quarterly for Exercise and
                Sport 51, 1: 110-121.

Sage, George H. and Loy, John W.
    1978   "Geographical mobility patterns of
                college coaches." Urban Life 7: 253-280.

Schmitt, Raymond L. and Leonard, Wilbert M., II.
    1986   "Immortalizing the self through sport."
                American Journal of Sociology 91, 5
                (March): 1088-1111.

Scott, J.
    1969   Athletes for Athletes. Other Ways Book
                Co. Oakland, CA.

Scott, J.
    1971   The Athletic Revolution. The Free Press.
                Glencoe, IL.

Seals, Greg and Hastings, Donald W.
    nd   "A revolution in pool-side paradigms:
                From Newton to Bernoulli."
                Sportwissenschaft (Forthcoming)

Smith, D. Randall, and Abbott, Andrew.
    1983   "A labor market perspective in the
                mobility of college football coaches."
                Social Forces 61, 3 (June): 1147-1167.

Smith, Ronald E., Smoll, Frank L., and Hunt, Earl.
    1977   "A system for the behavioral assessment
                of athletic coaches." Research Quarterly
                48, 2: 401-407.

Smoll, Frank L., Smith, Ronald E., Curtis, Bill, and
Hunt, Earl.
    1978   "Toward a mediational model of coach-
                player relationships." Research
                Quarterly 49, 4: 528-541.

Snyder, Eldon.
    1970   "Aspects of socialization in sport and physical education." Quest Monograph XIV (June): 1-7.

Stallman, R.K.
    1976   "Causes of high attrition in competitive swimming." Swimming Technique 13, 2 (Summer): 34-40.

Stebbins, Robert A.
    1970   "Career: The subjective approach." Sociological Quarterly 11, 1 (Winter): 32-49.

Stebbins, Robert A.
    1979   Amateurs: On the Margin Between Work and Leisure. Sage. Beverly Hills, CA.

Stevenson, Christopher L.
    1975   "Socialization effects of participation in sport: A critical review of the research." Research Quarterly 46, 3 (October): 287-301.

Stevenson, Christopher L.
    1976a   "Institutional socialization and college sport." Research Quarterly 47, 1 (March): 1-8.

Stevenson, Christopher L.
    1976b   "An alternative theoretical approach to sport socialization: A concept of institutional socialization." International Review of Sport Sociology 11, 1: 65-76.

Stevenson, Christopher L.
    1978   "A three nation study of institutional socialization and college sport." in Fernand Landry and William A.R. Orban. (Eds.) Sociology of Sport. Symposia Specialists, Inc. Miami, FL. pp. 79-86.

Stillwell, J.L.
    1979   "Why P.E. majors want to coach." Journal of Physical Education and Recreation 50, 9: 80.

Stone, Gregory P.
1955   "American sports: Play and display."
Chicago Review 9, 3 (Fall): 83-100.

Thornton, Karen Moe.
1981   "Workshop: Communication techniques." in
Robert M. Ousley (Ed.) World Clinic Year
Book. American Swimming Coaches
Association. Fort Lauderdale, FL. pp.
215-228.

Troup, John and Reese, Randy.
1983   A Scientific Approach to the Sport of
Swimming. Scientific Sports Enterprises,
Inc. Gainsville, FL.

Underwood, J.
1969   "The desperate coach." Sports
Illustrated 31, 9: 66-76.

Vroom, V.H. and Yetton, P.W.
1973   Leadership and Decision Making.
University of Pittsburgh Press.
Pittsburgh, PA.

Wadley, Bill.
1986   "College recruiting...with and without
financial aid choosing a college ...
making the right choice." ASCA
Newsletter (July/August): 27-28.

Walsh, J.M. and Carron, A.V.
1977   "Attitudes of volunteer coaches." Paper
presented at the meetings of the
Canadian Association of Sport Sciences,
Winnipeg.

Weiss, Maureen R. and Sisley, Becky L.
1984   "Where have all the coaches gone?"
Sociology of Sport Journal 1, 4
(December): 332-347.

Whitaker, Gail and Molstad, Susan.
1985   "Male coach/female coach: A theoretical
analysis of the female sport
experience." Journal of Sport and Social
Issues 9, 2 (Summer/Fall): 14-25.

168

Woodman, William F.
      1977   "An adapted model of the sport
                  participation process." Research
                  Quarterly 48, 2: 452-460.

Ziegler, S.G.
      1969   "A personality study of highly
                  successful and ideal coaches." Research
                  Quarterly 40: 299-304.

AUTHOR INDEX

Abbott,A. 54, 166
ASCA 5, 84, 153
Anderson,W.G. 61, 153, 155
Anselmi,K. 5, 153
Armistead,D. 56, 58, 72, 124, 153
Arnott,M. 79, 155

Bain,L. 153
Bales,R.F. 60, 153
Ball,D.W. 153, 160, 166
Barrette,G.T. 61, 153, 155
Bay,A. 28, 158
Beach,L.R. 157
Becker,H.S. 18, 154
Bennett,B.B. 81, 155
Betz,M. 5, 154
Biddle,B.J. 153
Blinde,E.M. 147, 154, 158
Boesch,J. 114, 154
Broderick,R. 154
Brown,B. 154
Bussard,R. 124, 154

Caccese,T.M. 44, 147, 154
Carron,A.V. 78, 81, 155, 160, 168
Cheffers,J.T.F. 61, 155
Chelladurai,P. 75, 78-79, 155
Chu,D. 142, 156
Clark,W. 163
Coakley,J.J. 48, 156
Coons,A.E. 157-159
Counsilman,J.E. 28, 156
Cratty,B.J. 156
Curtis,B. 166

Daland,P. 81, 156
Daniel,J.V. 164
Daniels,C.M. 156
Danielson,R.R. 78, 156
de B. Handley,L. 156
Decker,J.I. 136, 157

Drake,C.J. 156
Dummer,G. 117, 157
Edwards,H.H. 157
Eitzen,D.S. 164

Feltz,D. 158
Fiedler,D. 157
Fisher,C.A. 62, 157
Fleishman,E.A. 78, 157
Freas,S. 115, 157
Friedman,L. 107, 158

Gambril,D. 28, 33, 158
Geer,B. 154
Gehrke,N.J. 158
Glaser,N. 2, 158
Goffman,E. 14, 66, 158
Gould,D. 31, 64, 158
Greendorfer,S.L. 147, 154, 156, 158, 162

Haggerty,T.R. 78, 155
Halpin,A.W. 78, 159
Hannula,D. 38, 159
Hart,B.A. 44, 159
Hasbrook,C.A. 44, 159
Hastings,D.W. 28, 38, 65, 88, 159, 166
Haufler,S.E. 164
Hendry,L.B. 74-75, 78, 159-160
Heusner,W.W. 157
Hirsch,R.L. 157
Holmen,M.G. 44, 160
Horn,T.S. 158, 160
Horne,T. 160
Hrycaiko,D. 72, 162
Hughes,E.C. 2, 160
Hunt,E. 165

Ingham,A.G. 160
Ingram,D. 160

Jamieson,J. 165

Kelly,J.R. 15, 160
Kenyon,G. 2, 161
Klavora,P. 164

171

SUBJECT INDEX